The **Athene Series** assumes that those who formulate explanations of the way the world works need to know and appreciate the significance of basic feminist principles.

The growth of feminist research internationally has called into question almost all aspects of social organization in our culture. The **Athene Series** focuses on the construction of knowledge and the exclusion of women from the process—both as theorists and subjects of study—and offers innovative studies that challenge established theories and research.

ATHENE, the Olympian goddess of wisdom, was honored by the ancient Greeks as the patron of arts and sciences and guardian of cities. She represented both peace and war, the latter in its cognitive aspect. Her mother, Metis, was a Titan and presided over all knowledge. While pregnant with Athene, Metis was swallowed whole by Zeus. Some say this was his attempt to embody her supreme wisdom. The original Athene is thus twice born: once of her strong mother, Metis, and once more out of the head of Zeus. According to feminist myth, there is a "third birth" of Athene when she stops being an agent and mouthpiece of Zeus and male dominance, and returns to her original source: the wisdom of womankind.

DISCIPLINING SEXUALITY

Foucault, Life Histories, and Education

SUE MIDDLETON

FOREWORD BY MICHAEL W. APPLE

Teachers College, Columbia University
New York and London

Published by Teachers College Press, 1234 Amsterdam Avenue, New York, NY 10027

Library of Congress Cataloging-in-Publication Data

Middleton, Sue, 1947–
   Disciplining sexuality : Foucault, life histories, and education / Sue Middleton ; foreword by Michael W. Apple.
      p.   cm. — (Athene series)
   Includes bibliographical references and index.
   ISBN 0-8077-6292-X (cloth). — ISBN 0-8077-6291-1 (pbk.)
   1. Sex—Philosophy. 2. Sex customs—History. 3. Sex role—History. 4. Education—Philosophy. 5. Body, Human—Social aspects. 6. Foucault, Michel—Contributions in the philosophy of education. 7. Foucault, Michel—Contributions in feminist theory.
I. Title. II. Series.
HQ23.M48   1997
306.7′01—dc21   97-37208

ISBN 0-8077-6291-1 (paper)
ISBN 0-8077-6292-X (cloth)

Printed on acid-free paper
Manufactured in the United States of America

05 04 03 02 01 00 99 98   8 7 6 5 4 3 2 1

Contents

Foreword

When I was asked to write the Foreword to *Disciplining Sexuality*, I at first hesitated. Was I the wisest choice? After all, while I had analyzed the relationship between gender and teaching in some of my own work and had suggested that attempts at controlling both curricula and teaching had complex connections to the control of sexuality and the body, most of my work had not been about sexuality and the body. And even though I have sympathy with parts of a Foucauldian agenda, I have criticized some of the uses of such perspectives (Apple, 1993, 1996).

Yet, perhaps because of the fact that I am growing weary of the constant internecine battles among the multiple traditions of critical educational research, I thought that it actually would be wise for someone who *has* been critical of parts of the Foucault-inspired agenda in education to point to those volumes that do demonstrate what such a Foucauldian perspective—when used reflexively and appropriately—can in fact illuminate about the workings of power. It can indeed provide insights that are often missed in other critical approaches. Further, as you will see in the next section of this Foreword, Sue Middleton's construction of this approach resonates powerfully with memories and experiences that many educators and students have simply by living in those places called schools. Perhaps I can make this clear by sharing some of my own memories.

MEMORIES OF THE BODY

It was the first week of school. The summer heat not only dragged on, but seemed to intensify. By midday, when the students came into that classroom in P.S. 4 ("foursies" as it was called) after lunch, it was well over 100 degrees in the room. I personally was excited to be in that room; after all, this was my first week as a teacher, something I had looked forward to for as long as I could remember. Yet the heat was oppressive, a situation made much worse by the fact that P.S. 4 was housed in a building that was so old that most of the windows no longer opened. I made a decision. I took off my jacket and tie. This was not at all a wise move, it seemed. The principal made a habit of walking the halls and looking in on the classrooms. All of the doors to each classroom had windows so that what was going on inside could be seen. The door to my classroom was thrust open quickly by the principal. She berated me in front of the children for "daring to take off my tie." "What would the children think of teachers if we all did that, Mr. Apple?" Too embarrassed to say anything in response, I quickly put tie and jacket back on. The 42 mostly poor, inner city African-American and Latino/Latina children in that classroom said nothing either. But the message to them and to me was clear.

Fast forward a few years. I am now a "veteran" teacher, with a class of sixth graders in a small school in a rural area of the same state. I have been instructed to make certain that the school "dress code" is enforced to the letter, especially for "girls." Thus, when the 12–13 year old "girls" come into the classroom each day, I am to "inspect them." If I see anyone wearing a dress or skirt that was "at or above the knees," I am to have her kneel down on the floor near my desk. If the hemline does not touch the floor, she is to be sent to the school office where she will be sent home to change into something "more appropriate." She will not be admitted back into the school until this is done. The rule is intensely disliked by everyone in my classroom. The students and I discuss this in detail. It becomes a focal point of study of how what counts as appropriate attire, hair length, etc. change over the years. We prepare a pamphlet to present to the principal. We get in a bit of hot water at first, but the dress code is made more flexible. This entire incident, and the teaching that surrounded it, serves as an important lesson for these youth both on how ideas about "appropriateness" change over time and on how we can act to change them.

Both of the stories with which I begin this Foreword are true (or at least as true as my memory allows). Both are about the nature of institutional power and about the regulation and normalization of the body. In the first instance, it was the teacher—me—who was the subject of such practice. But the message was also for the children from that poverty stricken neighborhood. Bodies, including those of the teachers, must be controlled. In the second instance, it is the bodies of the female students that are policed. Male bodies in this instance are not subject to such action—although they are aggressively policed when they become too active and are seen to be "out of control."

Of course, there is nothing new in these stories. They speak to a much longer tradition in which student bodies, working class bodies, poor person's bodies, women's bodies, the bodies of gays and lesbians, are brought under control. There rightly is a burgeoning literature on these topics to demonstrate the long history of such "disciplining of the body." It is now widely known that the struggle over sports and physicality played a role in disciplining working class women and men. Dance halls where working class women frequented were also regulated and policed. (And I do mean this literally. Police were a very real physical presence there.) The regulation of the Black woman's and man's bodies and the myths generated to support such actions are too painful to repeat. Whether we recognize it overtly or not, the body is central to the exercise of power.

It speaks to the power of Sue Middleton's latest book that these kinds of memories are called forth. The fact that reading *Disciplining Sexuality* made me think of my own personal experiences as a teacher says something about the nature of what she has accomplished in this book. She has created a space where issues of everyday power that have too often been talked about in arcane and over-theorized ways can be connected to the lives of a large number of people who have gone to or worked in educational institutions. This is no small accomplishment. Middleton presents a Foucauldian perspective in a manner that is clear and unmystified. She demonstrates how the use of such a perspective can illuminate the way power works — negatively and positively — in daily events. And she does all this in a way that enables the reader to recognize why things we take for granted about sexuality and the body need to be rethought. In essence, we might say that what she has done is to give us a picture of "embodied theory." I mean this in two ways. She has presented a Foucauldian inspired approach in which the body is put back into theory. And she has done so in a way in which she, as an embodied historical person, becomes the lens in which the reader can "read" much that is taken for granted in cultural politics and schooling.

Rather than seeing the "disciplined body" inside and outside schools as passive and as having little agency, as some scholars in education who have been influenced by Foucault have done, Sue Middleton provides a more nuanced and a more active view. In many ways she is similar to Judith Butler, who argues that subjectification needs to be understood in two ways. It is both a form of domination *and* a process of activating the subject. Thus, subjection implies resistance. In Butler's words, "any mobilization against subjection will take subjection as its resource" (Butler, 1995, p. 246). As this book shows, Middleton would agree.

AGAINST HERESY

In a recent book of mine, *Cultural Politics and Education* (Apple, 1996), I suggest that there has been an overly defensive dismissal of "post" approaches by many leftist scholars and a much too rejectionist and essentializing dismissal of the many gains made by more "structural" traditions by postmodern and poststructural theorists. Instead of treating each other as something like enemies, I urge a different approach. I argue that we must let neo-marxist and postmodern and poststructural theories "rub against each other." Neither is to be ignored. Each has something of crucial importance to teach us.

Let me be clear. I do not wish to take an overly romantic position on this. Both theories are "postures toward knowledge and power that need one another." Yet they both also "stand in irreducible tension and cannot be cordially joined" (Kathy Ferguson, quoted in Tavares, 1997). However, I believe that this combination of need and tension is not bad, but is immensely productive. Rejectionist impulses from either side are less than helpful.

I say this for reasons both of deep political commitment and because of my respect for those who are teaching all of us about the possible limitations of aspects of some of the "critical" traditions many critical educators have come to accept. After all, since we are not in a church, we should not be worried about heresy. Yet, I do want to make an additional point here. All positions—be they neo-marxist, postmodern, or poststructural—have elements of what Gramsci would have called "good sense" and "bad sense" in them. Narrative perspectives that focus on voice, testimony, autobiography, memory, and so on are of exceptional importance. They carve out spaces for the embodied voices of the silenc*ed* (the stress on the last two letters is important here, since it signifies an active process of control, regulation, and policing) to be articulated. Yet, having said this, my own position is that here we need to take "post" theories about this as seriously as they deserve. That is, if we do have multiple identities, if we *are* all simultaneously sexed, gendered, classed, raced, aged, etc. in complicated and contradictory ways (see Haraway, 1989), this means that we must always reflexively examine the contradictory possibilities and power relations in our voices and positions—including the autobiographical voice. Thus, we need to remember that an identity politics based on, say, sexuality is also at times a class voice, a voice that comes from a position in the social and racial, and gender, divisions of paid and unpaid labor. This does not diminish its power or insight, but I hope that it does remind us that the task is to think *across* traditions, to simultaneously think political economy, cultural struggles, the body, and sexuality. Capillary power does not totally replace a focus on structural relations. Structural relations can never fully account for capillary power. As Bourdieu (1990) reminds us, "trespassing" is the primary path to progress.

Of course, I am not alone in making these claims. There is quite an extensive tradition within various "neo" and "post" writings and within various feminisms and postcolonialisms urging us to take *both* structural *and* poststructural insights seriously and to be as reflexive as possible about the contradictions within one's "voice." I wish to side with and ratify these insights, as does Sue Middleton in this and other works.

Foucault's theories of power, the body, sexuality, and desire have been subject to some quite important critiques (see, e.g., Stoler, 1995; Tavares, in press; Zipin, in press) of which those scholars who appropriate his theories should be very knowledgeable. Yet, they have also generated powerful new insights about micro-relations of power. There is no doubt in my mind that—used well and not employed simply to "diss" other analyses of power—they offer disciplined (pardon the play on words) insights that will enable us to see things in important new ways. In this book, Sue Middleton demonstrates how the use of Foucault can help us understand and act on disciplining processes of which anyone who has attended school in any nation will have powerful memories. The fact that she extends her discussion to deal insightfully with issues of censorship and pornography makes this book an even more thoughtful contribution.

Michael W. Apple
John Bascom Professor
University of Wisconsin, Madison

REFERENCES

Apple, Michael W. (1993). *Official knowledge.* New York: Routledge.

Apple, Michael W. (1996). *Cultural politics and education.* New York: Teachers College Press.

Bourdieu, Pierre. (1990). *In other words.* Stanford: Stanford University Press.

Butler, Judith. (1995). "Subjection, resistance, resignification." In John Rajchaman (Ed.), *The identity in question.* New York: Routledge.

Haraway, Donna. (1989). *Primate visions.* New York: Routledge.

Stoler, Ann. (1995). *Race and the education of desire.* Durham, NC: Duke University Press.

Tavares, Hannah. (1997). "Poststructural feminisms and alter-pedagogical tales." Unpublished paper, University of Wisconsin-Madison, Department of Educational Policy Studies.

Tavares, Hannah. (in press). "Review of *Race and the education of desire*," *Theory and Event.*

Zipin, Lew. (in press). "Emphasizing 'discourse' and bracketing people," in Thomas Popkewitz and Marie Brennan (Eds.), *Foucault's challenge: Discourse, knowledge, and power in education.* New York: Teachers College Press.

Acknowledgments

This book has grown from three separate projects, each of which has brought me into contact with many people who have shared their life stories, supported my work in various material or intellectual ways, and extended to me their friendship and encouragement.

Chapters One and Two were revised from a paper that I presented at the annual meeting of the American Educational Research Association in New York, April 1996: "Canes, Berets, and Gangsta Rap: Disciplining Sexuality in School, 1920–1995." I would like to thank the 75 teachers and former teachers who so generously shared their experiences and perspectives with me in the interviews that I excerpted in my paper. These were part of a wider collaborative project with Helen May—an oral history of educational ideas—and I would like to acknowledge Helen's friendship and support throughout this 3-year project. The wider project (of which the data used in this book are but a tiny part) was given initial funding by the University of Waikato Research Committee, which was later "topped up" by the University of Waikato School of Education's Research Committee. I would like to acknowledge the work of the developers of the NUD-IST software program, and the Help desk at QSR Corp Pty Ltd., La Trobe University, for making the analysis of my vast quantities of qualitative data so much simpler.

The reorientation of these accounts of "disciplining" sexuality in New Zealand schools towards the North American audiences to whom this book is addressed was facilitated by my visits in 1996 to the AERA conference in New York and to two Canadian universities. My visit to the Ontario Institute for Studies in Education was made possible by David Livingstone, Kari Dehli, and Roxanna Ng, and I thank them for their hospitality. I was also privileged to receive a Distinguished Visitor's Award at the Center for Research for Teacher Education and Development at the University of Alberta, Edmonton. Thanks to Jean Clandinin for organizing my visit, making me feel at home, and sharing work in progress. Thanks also to Andrea Borys and the doctoral students there for looking after my intellectual and recreational needs so well.

The stories of feminism and sex in Chapter Three were told to me in a context which now seems distant—that of the "second wave" of feminism in the early 1980s. This previously unpublished material completes the "publication in installments" of my doctoral thesis. These 12 women's stories about the dramas of their sex lives, to paraphrase one interviewee, in familial and educational settings from the 1950s to the early 1980s seemed too intimate to bring to the light of day until now. I thank them again for trusting me to use this sensitive material carefully.

The starting point for Chapter Four was a paper that I published in *Sites, 29* (1994)—a cultural studies journal based at Massey University. I thank the editors of *Sites* for permission to revise the original paper, entitled "Sex, Drugs and Bombs: Six Years on the Indecent Publications Tribunal." My 6 years on the tribunal were enriched by the friendship and intellectual stimulation of its members: Judge Richard Kearney, Rosemary Barrington, Waana Davis, Alistair Graham, Bill Hastings, Anne Holden, and Keri Hulme. I am particularly grateful to Peter Cartwright, the tribunal's final chairperson, for encouraging me to write the paper and for comments on earlier drafts.

All of these three projects have been brought about in the course of my employment at the University of Waikato. I thank my colleagues and students there—especially at the Department of Education Studies—for their friendship and support for my research and writing over the years. Noeline Alcorn, the dean of the School of Education, has been there for me as a professional mentor, literary critic, and personal friend. My wider network of academic friends and colleagues within and beyond New Zealand has kept me inspired through their e-mail and exchanges of papers, letters, and social engagements. In particular, I acknowledge the stimulation of continuing interchanges with Michael Apple, Madeleine Arnot, Rosemary du Plessis, Maxine Greene, Alison Jones, Geraldine McDonald, Liz McKinley, Kathleen Weiler, and Lyn Yates.

Most important, my husband, George, has kept me sane by loving me, and our 20-year-old daughter Kate has kept me feeling just a little bit young as I approach my 50th birthday.

Introduction

Early in 1996, a number of universities and other gateways to the Internet blocked off access to all the news groups subsumed under the header *alt.sex* and other sites of sexual information on the World Wide Web. As one academic expressed it, their reasoning was

> to avoid possible pornographic issues or uses of the Internet. Clearly, this was done to protect the female users of the net. However, such an act of protection may well be counterproductive, especially for those academics, such as myself, whose research is in the field of the body, sexuality, medicalisation and gay and lesbian studies. (de Ras, 1996, p. 136)

Fifteen years previously, in 1981, I was researching teachers of my own age. Speaking of university days in the mid-1960s, one of my interviewees said:

> I remember putting a hell of a lot more energy into my sex life
> and my emotional life than I ever did into my work, and really
> university was just a backdrop against which the dramas of my
> sex life were played out. All sorts of things that were anathema to
> my parents were played out.

Both of these speak of a mind–body split. They suggest a contradiction or conflict between the rational and bodily — or professional and erotic — dimensions of life in higher education (McWilliam & Jones, 1995). On the assumption that a study of this contradiction, and of sex and the body in education more generally, would be of great interest to students, I designed a course on "education and sexuality," which I have taught since 1993. Preparing my lectures and compiling the readings has demanded new teaching resources. Accordingly, I have mined my NUD-IST (electronic)[1] database and some earlier data — three research projects in all.[2] This book is the result.

In the course of hundreds of research interviews with teachers and former teachers — men and women of all ages — I have been told countless stories about the (male and female) body as an object of educational interventions and disciplinary practices in families, schools, and the wider society. A young woman teacher offered the following account of how, in 1994, she focused her curriculum on her students' bodies:

> I taught from music videos because I suddenly realized that the
> way my Pacific Islands students were dressing — their hairstyles,
> the way they spoke, everything — was coming from the music vid-
> eos in American films. They all wanted to be gangstas. . . . When
> I started my first job in this school, which has no uniform, the
> kids were actually wearing the stuff. Their hairstyles were from
> music videos and the way they talked with their bodies was all
> this rap gangsta kind of stuff.

A middle-aged man described the disciplining of students' bodies in a Catholic boys high school in the 1950s:

> There was a thing about hair being cut straight — *straight backs* —
> you weren't allowed them. A few of us, who were getting into
> that rebellious age, got them. During the day we were all picked
> out one by one and taken up to the discipline master, who was
> waiting in the place where the priests used to live. I remember go-
> ing up the tower, knock, knock, and into a dark room. And there
> he was with a chair in the middle, ready with all his haircutting
> material and he cut my hair.

And an older woman told the following story about being a student in a
coeducational secondary school in the 1930s:

> We were divided into four houses for sports. At the end of every
> month marks were credited to your house. They had a very strict
> prefect system. If you weren't a prefect you couldn't walk up the
> main steps into the school, you had to go around through the
> back entrance. The prefects had to examine the uniforms every
> Monday morning to see if they were the correct length. And boys
> and girls had a separate playground, of course.

Reading all of these, and thousands of similar accounts, I am struck by
their compatibility with Foucault's later works (1977, 1980a, 1980b,
1982) — his empirical studies of the mechanisms of power in the institutions
which characterize modern Western societies.[3] Intending his own empirical
studies as exemplars rather than as providing an overarching theory, he
urged social researchers to focus not so much on the global, but on the local
and particular. We should, he said, research the apparatuses of power less
from the top-down point of view of policymakers, and more from the
bottom-up perspective of everyday life within the architectural spaces of
institutions such as prisons, hospitals, asylums, and schools:

The analysis in question should not concern itself with the regulated and legitimate forms of power in their central locations; with the general mechanisms through which they operate, and the continual effects of these. On the contrary, it should be concerned with power at its extremities, in its ultimate destinations, with those points where it becomes capillary, that is, in its more regional and local forms of institutions. (1980b, p. 96)

He urged us to study the everyday workings of power in its "capillary form of existence, the point where power reaches into the very grain of individuals, touches their bodies and inserts itself into their actions and attitudes, their discourses, learning processes and everyday lives" (p. 39).

In my research, my teaching, and my reflections on administrative practice, I have found this line of inquiry useful. For some time I have wanted to explore in depth the empirical and pedagogical possibilities of Foucault's framing of power, the body, sexuality, and schooling. To what extent is it fruitful as an object of study? How can it help educators understand, and act creatively, in the institutions in which we and our students study and teach? What can it tell us about the bodily constraints and possibilities that we experience in the course of our everyday lives in educational settings?

My emphasis, then, is on the conditions of possibility—historical, political, cultural, economic, and biographical—for what Maxine Greene (1995) has referred to as "releasing the educational imagination." Can Foucauldian empirical studies of the mechanisms of power assist us in this? Is the process that I call the disciplining of sexuality in educational settings—schools and cyberspace—in some ways productive of educational thought? Some have argued that Foucault's approach is antithetical to such a task. They point out that "Readers of Foucault sometimes emerge with the dismaying impression of a paranoid hyper-rationalist system in which the strategies—technologies—programs of power merge into a monolithic regime of social subjection" (Gordon, 1980, p. 246). Similarly, but somewhat more bluntly, Camille Paglia (1995) talks of "today's slag heaps of bombastic, Foucault-inspired rubbish that predicate the body as passive to a lumpish something called power!" (p. 340).

The center of interest in this book, as in my research and teaching, is human agency. As a teacher of university courses in education, I seek an alternative to flat map approaches in which students are positioned outside the theoretical typologies they are studying. Clandinin and Connelly (1995) explain the top-down way student teachers often encounter educational theories, policies, and research: "For the most part a rhetoric of conclusions is packaged and transmitted via the conduit to the teacher's pre-formed knowledge landscape" (p. 9). In an effort to position students inside what they are studying, I have experimented with contextualized personal narratives. In some of my courses this approach has included the opportunity for students to contextualize their own schooling historically and sociologically (Middleton, 1993a, 1993b, 1995). However, in a "sex" course, personal disclosures—diaries, autobiographical writing, displays of personal relics or artifacts—seem inappropriate, since most of us do not consider the "dramas of our sex lives" to be matters for public display. "Confessional" pedagogies can be voyeuristic (Luke & Gore, 1992b; Orner, 1992; Middleton, 1993a).

I want to introduce students to educational ideas and policies—especially about the body and sexuality—as teachers and students experience, choose, and live them in everyday settings. Educational life-histories—when contextualized historically, politically, and sociologically—can help student teachers to deconstruct the constraints and possibilities of their own and others' lives and to view teachers as active and creative educational theorists who do not merely mimic what has gone before. Rather, they create new amalgams of the theories and concepts that they encounter in the course of their professional lives and create pedagogies and educational strategies which are uniquely their own.

In this book I draw on Foucault in combination with life-history narratives from my research interviews and autobiographical experience in order to "excavate and analyze some of the key concepts that provide the bedrock of contemporary educational practice" (Ball, 1990b, p. 6) in secondary schools and higher education. Throughout, I address the following questions:

- How have the changing theories about sexuality that have gained ascendancy in the twentieth century in Western English-speaking countries inscribed themselves on the (female and male) bodies of teachers and students?
- How have changing ideas about sex (as a quality of bodies) been enmeshed in the various pedagogies and disciplinary practices of schools?
- How have their sexual/bodily experiences in education been formative of teachers' educational ideas?
- What educational questions are being raised by the disciplining of sexuality as educational environments move into cyberspace?
- What implications do all of these questions have for teacher educators at the end of the millenium?

I research, teach, and write in New Zealand. The stories I tell contain details of lives, schools, and policies with aspects that may seem foreign to overseas readers. Yet I ask you to consider them as local variants of broad common experiences, for in the past one hundred years New Zealand's shores have been washed by many of the same tides and currents of educational thought, conceptualizations of sex, and political movements as have those of the United States, Canada, Britain, and Australia. I ask you to use the details of our foreign-ness to make strange the taken-for-granted in your own country's disciplinary practices. As one American reader of New Zealand work recently put it, many of the "current debates in New Zealand . . . bear a striking resemblance to U.S. discussions" (Kirsch, 1995, p. 727). She commented that consideration of the New Zealand situation can provide American readers with "some mirror images of current debates. However, since the stakes are defined differently, it is easier to see the underlying issues without becoming caught up in the rhetoric of the day" (p. 727).

As an example of our common experience: In New Zealand as elsewhere many have characterized present-day education policies as dominated by New Right theories. They say that the liberal/progressive ideals of the post–World War II years—in which education was conceptualized as the route to democracy and equality of opportunity—have, in the late twentieth century, become politically subordinate to commercial values such as the maximization of profit and technical efficiency. Schools "are called upon to create skills and no longer ideals—so many doctors, so many teachers in a given discipline, so many engineers, so many administrators, etc." (Lyotard, 1984, p. 48). Educational criteria have become subordinate to commercial ideals such as "efficiency" or "performativity" and are oriented "to supply the system with players capable of acceptably fulfilling their roles at the pragmatic posts required by its institutions" (p. 48).

Since the late 1980s, such arguments have surfaced in the United States (Apple, 1996a; Secada, 1989), Canada (Livingstone, 1987), Australia (Lingard, Knight, & Porter, 1993), Britain (Ball, 1994; Flude & Hammer, 1990), and New Zealand (Codd, 1996; Grace, 1990; Lauder & Wylie, 1990; Peters & Marshall, 1996). The ideals of progressivism—that education is to further the causes of democracy and equality—are seen as being in retreat. In some of these studies, Foucault's work is used to highlight the dominance of what one critic called "busnocratic rationality" over democratic or progressive educational values (Peters & Marshall, 1996).

Writing from Australia, Erica McWilliam (1995) reports how her student teachers react to the pessimism pouring from the mouths and computers of critical educational theorists: "Critical teacher educators are increasingly perceived as conveying little more than a litany of complaints about the very sort of contemporary practice student teachers have to imitate" (p. 68). Like her, I would describe my "overwhelming concern" as one of "helping my students to understand the power relations in which teachers work"—and in which they as students study—"without being defeated by them" (p. 134).

Chapter One begins by my introducing Foucault's approach to writing "the history of the present" and his concepts of discipline and sexuality. It then explores questions of (female and male) embodiment in secondary schools today—from both the top-down perspective of policymakers and the bottom-up point of view of men and women teachers of all ages whom I have interviewed. In Chapter Two I use the same database to construct an account of disciplining sexuality in secondary schools from 1920 to the mid-1980s. In both these chapters I am interested in how dominant and subordinate discourses concerning education and sexuality are intertwined.

Chapter Three draws on different data to explore the sex education and bodily experiences of 12 feminist teachers, who were all of the post–World War II generation, as—in their families, schools, and wider social settings—they experienced childhood in the 1950s, puberty in the 1960s, sexual relationships and feminism during the "sexual revolution" in the 1970s. In Chapter Four I take further this theme of the sexual revolution and draw on my 6-year involvement in the formation and implementation of policies concerning the censorship of sexual materials. Although located outside formal education, these have broad implications for it. As Foucault advised, "it may be wise not to take as a whole the rationalization of society or of culture, but to analyze such a process in several fields, each with reference to a fundamental experience" (Dreyfus & Rabinow, 1982, p. 210). The chapter concludes with speculations on the disciplining of virtual bodies in cyberspace.

Throughout, this book transgresses some conventions of academic writing. I seldom write from the stance of a disengaged and detached observer, but make visible the settings in which my ideas are being generated. As teachers and prospective teachers, we are positioned inside that which is our object of study—education. My own intellectual production, including the researching and writing of this book, takes place in—is both constrained and enabled by—the very power relations which are its object of study. I reveal my "insider" positioning for pedagogical—as well as substantive—reasons, and I shall make these explicit in the book's conclusion.

In the course of the twentieth century, in schools and in cyberspace, how have educational theories—in interaction with ideas about sexuality—shaped, constrained, and made possible the details of our own and others' "embodiment" as children and parents, as students and teachers, as activists, partners, and lovers?

CHAPTER ONE

The Present as History

I begin this historical exploration of disciplining sexuality in the present—or as close to it as the processes of researching and writing will allow. I see my task as being "to seek out the new, that which is coming to birth in the present—a present that most of us are unable to see because we see it through the eyes of the past, or through the eyes of a 'future' that is a projection of the past" (Sheridan, 1980, p. 195). How can we write of the "now"? Writing research is always/already in and about the past: Our data are interviews or field notes which have been completed; the precise events discussed in them have happened; and interviewees' thinking and circumstances will continually change. The process of writing up research is one of transfixing ephemera: I write, press the delete key, and continually rewrite as my ideas change. Fluid thoughts are frozen by print into snapshots of moments past.

To write a history of the present in Foucault's (1982) sense, "We have to know the historical conditions which motivate our conceptualization. We need a historical awareness of our present circumstance" (p. 209). Rather than regard the present teleologically—as the end-point of a steady progress towards liberation or enlightenment—we should be less ambitious, he argued, and study "the present as the form of a particular kind of domain of rationality" (p. 241) or "regime of truth." What I am writing about are broad continuities and discontinuities in the webs of intersecting discourses that make up the regimes of truth—the theories/practices, the power-knowledges in educational settings—with respect to the bodies of teachers and students. A discursive regime in which I—as a teacher educator, an educational researcher/writer, and a university "middle manager"—am also enmeshed, write, and am written into the "cultural archive" (Middleton, 1993a; Said, 1993; D. Smith, 1987, 1990). As Gyatri Spivak (1990) has argued, the "institutional responsibility" of those of us who do this work "is of course to offer a responsible critique of the production of the knowledge we teach even as we teach it" (p. 103).

I shall begin by briefly exposing the nuts and bolts—the mechanics—of the research process. Second, I shall explain the main conceptual tools I am using in this empirical analysis—Foucault's notion of discipline in general and, as an item on his broader agenda, his framing of sexuality as an object for empirical research in education. Third, drawing on this, I present a thematic reading of my 75 life-history interviews—of the practices of disciplining sexuality in the secondary schools of the postreform era (1984–1995).[1] In the fourth and final section I identify from my data key discourses concerning discipline and sexuality as lived out and described by my interviewees with respect to their experiences in present-day secondary schools. This serves as a launching pad for Chapter Two, in which I excavate[2] the traces of these discourses in the sedimented layers of my interview data concerning the years from 1920 to the mid-1980s.

WRITING A HISTORY OF THE PRESENT

Foucault did his own research in libraries: He explored the archival legacy of past institutions—hospitals, clinics, asylums, and prisons. His data were already in written form: case histories, personal diaries, letters, institutional reports, textbooks used in professional training, and handbooks used in clinical practices (Macey, 1995; Miller, 1993). These professional/institutional records were created when people became objects of professional/administrative surveillance; when they were "seen," diagnosed or classified, disciplined or "normalized" by those working in the apparatuses of power. This happened when they were convicted of crimes, were diagnosed as mad or bad, normal or pathological. As objects of social regulation, people became "cases" and were written about. These written traces were Foucault's data. He did not do or write about the kind of qualitative studies in which sociologists and others now engage—data that is produced in interviews specific to the research encounters.

Modern technology allows us as qualitative researchers to do rapid and multiple readings of large numbers of interview transcripts. While the structure of life-history interviews—and the transcripts which fix them in print—is, by definition, (more or less) chronological and linear (albeit meandering like a river); computer databases can help us to view across multiple interviews and thereby to draw cross sections of the regimes of truth of a particular time and place. The NUD-IST program has helped me to read across 1,500 pages of text—transcripts of 75 life-history interviews—and to create textual snapshots of slices of time. This and the following chapter together constitute a textual collage of four slices of time and provide access to their sequential and concurrent regimes of truth with respect to education and sexuality/the body, as my interviewees describe their enactment in the everyday disciplinary practices of the secondary schools that they attended as pupils and in which they taught.

While my life-history interview data provide a view from the bottom up, I also use key policy documents to add a view from the top. In these two chapters I give equal weight to the voices of legislators, institutional policymakers, researchers, "grand theorists," and "ordinary" teachers who talk about their own secondary schooling and teaching practice. Several writers (e.g., Middleton, 1993a; Said, 1993) have used the musical metaphor of *counterpoint* to describe the intent in such writing, in which themes and arguments are interwoven rather than strictly cumulative:

> In the counterpoint of western classical music, various themes play off one another, with only a provisional privilege being given to any particular one; yet in the resulting polyphony there is concert and order, an organised interplay that derives from the themes, not from a vigorous melodic or formal principle outside the work. (Said, 1993, p. 59)

Composing these chapters is like conducting a choir that includes many voices singing different notes and tunes—sometimes in harmony, sometimes as a cacophony. It is a jazz choir with some wild improvisations, but there is an underlying chordal "grammar," and together the voices weave a coherent score. I draw on the many files and texts from my personal archive—policy documents, the writings of other academics, snippets from previous writings, electronic and manilla folder databases of interview transcripts, and, at times, snatches of my own past and present location. And looking at all of these through Foucauldian spectacles I read them otherwise:

> As we look back at the cultural archive, we begin to re-read it not univocally but *contrapuntally*, with a simultaneous awareness both of the metropolitan history that is narrated and of those other histories against which (and together with which) the dominating discourse acts. (Said, 1993, p. 59)

This approach offers a more complex alternative to the pessimism of those who see today's schools as crushed by the hegemonic weight of New Right conservatism and technocracy. Political orthodoxies, although powerful, are never monolithic. There are always oppositions, alternatives, resistances, and creativities. Many policy analyses—from the Left and the Right—have relied so heavily on the reading of policy texts that their writings conceptualize teachers and students as puppets whose strings are pulled at the whim of those who are seen as possessing power over others. How are the educational and wider social theories of today's policymakers lived out by teachers and students in schools? Conversely, how do teachers' and students' ideas, resistances, and everyday behaviors shape policy decisions? How is history "written" on the bodies of teachers and students? And how do everyday school disciplinary practices "sexualize" our bodies?

DISCIPLINING FOUCAULT

Let me begin with a brief personal anecdote from a slightly earlier time, for I have long lived inside, and been perplexed by, the object of study that Foucault framed for us to research—the apparent tension in schools between education and discipline, freedom and control. In 1970 I began my first teaching job in a secondary school. Good teaching, I believed, on the strength of a stiff dose of educational psychology at teachers college, involved being able to craft connections between educational knowledge (the given content of the syllabus) and where the kids were at in their interests and stages of development. If children were kept busy on activities which both interested and challenged (but did not overtax) them, they would develop as autonomous, self-disciplined learners. However, although I worked late most nights on my lesson plans and what we called our "B.O.s" (behavioural objectives), it became increasingly clear that teaching—initiating students into the disciplines of rational inquiry and modes of aesthetic expression—was only a small part of what was required of me.

I seemed to spend much of my working day on activities of surveillance and discipline—making sure that pupils were present at allocated times in specified spaces, ensuring that socks and hair ribbons conformed with uniform regulations, and punishing those who failed to comply. I wrote records of my students' presence and absence, their adherence to behavioural norms, and their ratings on numerical scales of achievement and intelligence. At times the activity that I thought was the core of my chosen profession—educating—seemed to become marginalized or displaced by the processes of watching, regulating, standardizing, and normalizing students, and writing the results on official forms. My own compliance with the norms expected of teachers was monitored by inspectors, who graded me according to a hierarchical scale and placed my score alongside those of my peers on a normal curve. Education (learning the processes of autonomous and rational inquiry) seemed subordinate to its antithesis—obedience, compliance, conformity.

Many years later, as a graduate student, I studied the government's education policies of the time and found that these were centered on ideals of freedom, autonomy, and diversity. In 1983 I discovered Foucault's work on a trip to a conference in Australia. His account of the dilemmas of teaching encapsulated my experience beautifully:

> The general judicial form that guaranteed a system of rights that were egalitarian in principle was supported by these tiny, everyday, physical mechanisms, by all those systems of micropower that are essentially non-egalitarian and asymmetrical that we call the disciplines. (1977, p. 222)

For Foucault, the school was one of many sites that needed to be studied as part of a broader research agenda on the practices—the mechanisms—of "disciplinary power" that had gradually been developed in various institutions in Western societies since the eighteenth century as practical ways of handling demographic and technological changes. From the eighteenth century, technologies for the rationalized, bureaucratized, and professionalized surveillance and administration of daily life had gradually replaced the preindustrial feudal systems which relied on the personality, "divine right," and bodily presence of the sovereign and his/her delegated agents.

While some liberal/progressive (teleological) histories had tended to construe the development of Western representative democracies as a triumphal procession towards liberty and enlightenment, Foucault's archival studies of asylums, hospitals, prisons, and other institutions of disciplinary power led him to read history differently. Viewing freedom and subjection as flip sides of the same coin—as complementary rather than contradictory—he argued that "The Enlightenment,[3] which discovered the liberties, also invented the disciplines" (1977, p. 222). The democratic forms of government characteristic of Western capitalist states rested on the ideal (or fantasy) of individual rational autonomy—the core Enlightenment value. Yet the social order required citizens who were not only autonomous and free, but also both economically productive and politically subjected (rendered governable). As products of the Enlightenment, institutions of public schooling straddle this contradiction. Children in school learn to be both autonomous and governable—free and subjected.

Foucault's archival research (1977; 1980b) showed how within modern nation-states the population is governed by surveillance, classification, and normalization by professional, managerial, and administrative "experts." Pedagogy (the science of teaching) was developed alongside, and in interaction with, other professional knowledges (or disciplines) such as medicine, psychology, psychiatry, demography, and criminology. The professional ways of knowing (or discourses) developed within institutions such as hospitals, prisons, and schools, which were articulated to what

Dorothy Smith (1990) was later to call the "apparatuses of ruling." For example, most children are born within the medical system; are monitored in infancy by health and professional and welfare organizations; in kindergartens and schools they are categorized as "bright" or "dull," "normal" or "pathological," and may come under surveillance by psychologists, psychiatrists, or criminal justice professionals. The examinations to which individuals are subjected result in case records, which "fix" our identities in writing (on paper or in electronic databases), and these records may be passed from one disciplinary institution to another:

> The examination that places individuals in a field of surveillance also situates them in a network of writing; it engages them in a whole mass of documents that capture and fix them. The procedures of examination [are] accompanied . . . by a system of intense registration and of documentary accumulation. A "power of writing" [is] constituted as an essential part in the mechanisms of discipline. (Foucault, 1977, p. 189)

Like blood in the tiny capillaries of the human body, the disciplinary knowledges of professionals — articulated to the powers of government — flow through the conduits of intersecting professional networks, information systems, and social institutions.

For example, within schools the bodies of individuals are subjected to the *panoptic* (all-seeing) gaze: "A relation of surveillance, defined and regulated, is inscribed at the heart of the practice of teaching, not as an additional or an adjacent part of it, but as a mechanism that is inherent in it and which increases its efficiency" (Foucault, 1977, p. 141). This "relation of surveillance" — so central in teachers' everyday work — includes monitoring the spatial locations of students (where they may be and with whom they may mix); the postures students may assume within their allocated spaces inside and outside the classroom (static or moving, sitting in rows or in groups, in desks or on the floor, etc.); and the standardization of their dress (in some schools, even their underwear).

Foucault's concept of discipline, then, includes a view of the disciplines as the professional and administrative bodies of knowledge by which we, as teachers and students, are categorized, classified, or otherwise "known." Included in this are the criteria — psychological, for example — that teachers use to measure a student's success, growth, maturity, behavior, and so forth. It also includes the standards by which schools and teachers are assessed by authorities such as school inspectors or New Zealand's Education Review Office — efficiency and effectiveness among them — and the overarching theoretical rationale (or discourse) which holds these together. And, of course, it also includes the criteria by which educational research —

such as that in this book — is rendered acceptable (or not) to other academics, publishers, and students! In addition to the power-knowledges (bodies of knowledge or academic/professional disciplines), Foucault's concept of discipline encompasses such everyday discipline as routines, dressage, or drills, as well as the classifications of time (timetables, routines) and the design, compartmentalizations, and allocations of "cellular" space that are characteristic of institutions such as schools. As Paul Patton (1979) summarized it, discipline

> breaks down complex multiplicities into simple units . . . carefully repartitioned in a basically cellular space: for each individual a place and for each emplacement an individual. It breaks down activities and actions into simple, momentary movements, thus allowing their control and ordering through routines and timetables. (p. 121)

Foucault identified sexuality as a key theme to study from the many items on his agenda for researching the broader workings of disciplinary power across the separate but intersecting professions and institutions of modern societies. Its strategic importance in the workings of power lay in the fact that sexuality "concerns characteristics that are at the intersection between the discipline of the body and the control of the population" (Giddens, 1982, p. 219). Foucault's (1980a) account of this is worth quoting in some detail:

> One of the great innovations in the techniques of power in the eighteenth century was the emergence of "population" as an economic and political problem: population as wealth, population as manpower or labor capacity, population balanced between its own growth and the resources it commanded. Governments perceived that they were not dealing simply with subjects, or even with a "people," but with a "population," with its specific phenomena and its peculiar variables: birth and death rates, life expectancy, fertility, state of health, frequency of illnesses, patterns of diet and habitation. All these variables were situated at the point where the characteristic movements of life and the specific effects of institutions intersected. . . . At the heart of this economic and political problem of population was sex: it was necessary to analyze the birthrate, the age of marriage, the legitimate and illegitimate births, the precocity and frequency of sexual relations, the ways of making them fertile or sterile, the effects of unmarried life or of the prohibitions, the impact of contraceptive practices. (pp. 25–26)

Within this framing, sexuality is conceptualized as an object of administrative surveillance and regulation. If, as Foucault suggests, researchers study the theories/practices of this surveillance and regulation, our objects of study are certain scientific disciplines (power-knowledges) in their institu-tional/clinical settings. These include social science disciplines such as de-mography and sociology; medical discourses such as sociobiology and eu-genics; procedures for the regulation of access to abortion, contraception, and sexual information; the rules of alliance concerning marriage and di-vorce; and the definitions and policing of "deviant" sexual behaviours. These professional/administrative disciplines perform the function, as Dorothy Smith (1990) explains, of "transposing the actualities of people's lives into the conceptual currency with which they can be governed" (p. 11). In this Foucault saw the school as a key site to study. Alan Sheridan (1980) summarizes his argument as follows:

> With the nineteenth century, society increasingly developed mechanisms for policing the individual's behaviour. The school was one of the most important sites for the play of power — knowledge; the sexuality of school children was of paramount interest to all those concerned with education, from the architects who designed the buildings to the teachers who taught in them. (p. 172)

There is a large body of historical research that documents how in various Western countries, within the family and the school, as in the wider society, it has been customary to classify human bodies as male or female and to orient a child's upbringing around this binary distinction. There are biologists who have argued that the rigidity of this binary is cultural rather than natural, for nature constructs a continuum. Among newborn babies, between the poles of what count culturally as normal male and female, are various forms of hermaphroditism and other genetic and physiological ambiguities. However, argued Foucault (1980c), "it was a very long time before the postulate that a hermaphrodite must have a sex — a single true sex — was formulated. For centuries, it was quite simply agreed that her-maphrodites had two" (p. vii). In medieval times, he argued, hermaphro-dites could choose at the age of marriage whether to maintain or to change the sexuality to which their parents had assigned them at birth. Gradually doctors abandoned their idea that in some individuals the two sexes were mingled and saw their task as "deciphering the true sex that was hidden beneath ambiguous appearances" (p. viii). By the midnineteenth century, sexology as a regulative science sought "not only to establish the true sex of hermaphrodites but also to identify, classify, and characterize the different types of perversions" (p. xii). Intolerant of sexual ambiguities, Western cultures usually force all bodies into this binary divide through surgical and other medical interventions (Fausto-Sterling, 1993; Foucault, 1980c; Gilbert, 1996; Tuana, 1989).

Throughout the educational histories of Western countries, male and female bodies have been subjected in schools to normalizing practices which reinforce this opposition. Girls and boys were allocated different (and often unequal) spaces within school buildings and grounds, were subjected to different curricula and regimes of punishment, and were required to dress and deport themselves according to conventional norms of masculinity and femininity. There is now a substantial literature in which feminists and other social historians have studied these conventional norms, how they have varied for different social classes and "races" (Davis, 1981), and how they have changed over time (Fry, 1985; Olssen, 1981; Tennant, 1986; Walkowitz, 1980).

What guidelines, then, does such a Foucauldian position provide for my present inquiry? To read my data—my archive—through Foucauldian spectacles, I must, he wrote, "ask not the big theoretical questions of What is power? and Where does power come from?" Instead, he argued, we should focus on "the little question, What happens?" which, although "flat and empirical," allows us to scrutinize a much more "complex configuration of realities" (1982, p. 217). What, then, are the practices for disciplining male and female bodies in the schools of the 1990s? How are these articulated to particular educational or wider social theories (or regimes of truth)? And how do contemporary educational and sexual discourses combine to write themselves on the bodies of students and teachers in the educational and disciplinary practices of everyday life in today's schools?

CORPORATE BODIES?: TODAY'S SCHOOLS

The teachers whom I interviewed had much to say about life in schools under the present regime of truth, and I have structured their accounts of disciplining sexuality according to three themes: the politics of clothing and appearance, questions of the allocations and deployment of school spaces by girls and boys, and contemporary technologies for the management of students' behavior. Although these events were experienced in—and the stories were told about—various New Zealand locations, my travels and readings have told me that they are recognizable to my readers in Australia, Britain, Canada, and the United States. However, because there are points of detail about our New Zealand system that may be unfamiliar to some, I begin with a very brief overview of the recent restructuring of the New Zealand school system.

Educational Reforms—Views from the Top

The beginnings of New Zealand's present regime of truth in educational policy were signalled in 1984 by the election of the fourth Labor government, although the mechanics of the restructuring process did not get under way until 1989. Following recommendations in the Picot Report (Taskforce to Review Educational Administration, 1987), the government devolved responsibility for many educational decisions from central government authorities to boards of trustees, which were composed of parents, staff, and (in secondary schools only) student representatives. Labor's policies embodied contradictions between the atomized individualism of a free market economic vision and a centralized "socialist" conceptualization of equity. While Labor's New Right economic vision conceptualized the population as being comprised of atomized, competitive, acquisitive individuals, its equity policies viewed New Zealand society as being composed primarily of groups. These policies were based on the idea that certain groups, through no fault of their own, had been educationally disadvantaged and were therefore owed compensation. Within this discourse, schools were viewed as sites for effecting compensatory justice (Middleton, 1992a; 1992b).

The powers and responsibilities of each board of trustees were listed in school charters, which contained details of a school's broad objectives and specific goals. Some of these, including the equity objectives, were required by the government to be included and were nonnegotiable. Every school's "policies and practices" had to "seek to achieve equality of educational outcomes for both sexes, for rural and urban students; for students from all religions, ethnic, cultural, social, family and class backgrounds, and for all students irrespective of their ability or disability" (Ministry of Education, 1988, p. 8). Honoring the 1840 Treaty of Waitangi—which guaranteed equal rights to Maori (the indigenous Polynesian population) and Pakeha (white) settlers was also a salient equity objective. With respect to gender roles and embodied sexuality, schools were to assume responsibility for promoting equitable educational outcomes for both sexes, to develop equal opportunity objectives, to provide nonsexist role models for students, to develop nonsexist curricula, to have an equal employment opportunity policy, and to create an environment free of sexual harassment. Schools' attempts to meet their stated goals, including the equity objectives, were to be monitored by the Educational Review Office (ERO)—a clear example of Foucault's concept of the "power of examination."

The 1980s and 1990s saw a struggle between central and local authorities for the control of schools. During the 1990 general election campaign, Lockwood Smith—who was to become the minister of education in the

1990–1996 National government — announced that he would make the equity clauses optional on the grounds that Labor's equity policies were "Orwellian social engineering" (Alton-Lee & Densem, 1992; Leahy, 1996; Middleton, 1992b). Despite an outcry from feminists and Maori, the National government — backed by social conservatives (e.g., Irwin, 1996) — argued that enforcing a verbal "political correctness" on communities was contrary to the spirit of devolution and that questions of human rights (such as freedom from sexual harassment and racial discrimination) would continue to be guaranteed by central government's human rights legislation under which students and their parents could sue their school boards. New Zealand's 1977 Human Rights Commission Act and other statutes had already, they said, prohibited discrimination on grounds of sex, marital status, race, religion, and disability (Wilson, 1992). Sodomy had been decriminalized in 1987, and in 1993 the categories of sexual orientation and age were added to the Human Rights Commission legislation. The National government saw these, rather than school charters, as guarantees of equal opportunity to all students.

As I write (January 1997), the debate over the new subject syllabi which the National government is introducing under the rubric of its National Curriculum Framework (Ministry of Education, 1993) is bringing a strong tone of social conservatism into the political/educational scene. This is being directly imported from Britain and — resonant also of American debates (Paglia, 1995) — views requirements to address works by women and Maori in, say, the English syllabus, as diluting the quality of the academic/literary canon offered in schools (Cazden, 1992; Peters & Marshall, 1996; Snook, 1996). In addition, there are conservative religious groups who oppose multiculturalism and feminism (as "paganism"), but — after a brief period of sympathetic hearings from a conservative minister of education in the mid-1980s (Openshaw, 1983; Ryan, 1988) — these have not attained the political power that they have in the United States (Klatch, 1987). Despite some protests, the national curriculum documents still contain some, albeit weak, statements that (gender and cultural) inclusiveness is mandatory (Alton-Lee & Densem, 1992; Leahy, 1996). On the basis of my travels and my reading, and despite the lack of empirical data to back up my opinion, I would hazard a guess that New Zealanders' attitudes toward sex education and toward the discussion of sexual and moral questions in the classroom are in general more permissive than those across the spectrums of public schooling in Britain and in the United States (Apple, 1996a, 1996b; Paglia, 1995; Strossen, 1995).

This was the "present" of New Zealand's education policies at the time my interviews were conducted and at the time of writing — as viewed from the top by both the decision makers who wrote the policy texts and the academic critics who responded from various shades of the political spectrum. But what is the view from the playgrounds and classrooms? What are the disciplinary practices in the schools of the late twentieth century? How are the (male and female) bodies of teachers and students inscribed by the present regime of truth in the everyday micropractices of today's schools? Those who were interviewed had a great deal to say about questions of embodiment: the surveillance of their dress, the ways in which sexual matters could be and were spoken about, the differential distribution of sexed/gendered bodies in space, and technologies for the regulation of students' behavior.

In this and the following chapter I have indicated age by including the birth dates of interviewees; it can be useful to know whether a comment comes from a beginning or an experienced teacher. All names given to interviewees are fictitious.

Clothing Politics

Despite a deregulated climate with respect to formal dress codes for teachers, many of those whom I interviewed described ways in which what they wore to school was influenced by the normalizing gazes of their school communities, other teachers, and their students. The new devolved administrative structures have made schools more porous than they used to be in absorbing the expectations and values of their communities. This can influence how teachers dress. Maureen McWilliam (b. 1973) began her teaching career in the mid-1990s in an intermediate (junior high) school whose parents were predominantly from business and professional occupations. She described how the ethos of the business and professional world was inscribing itself on the bodies of the teachers:

> This intermediate is very much control orientated. Everything is
> orientated towards the child, but it's very much in terms of stream-
> ing the child into opportunities. Right down to the clothes, even
> to the colors used in the clothing. It's very bold, black, white. The
> staff were very much into power dressing and I found it really
> scary.

Several women said that the sexualizing gaze of male students influenced how they dressed for work. For some this required concealment of the body. For example, Julie King (b. 1969) was careful not to appear "provocative" to her mainly Pacific Island students: "I deliberately don't wear tight clothes. I'm very conscious about what I'm wearing. I wear quite baggy clothes, or if I have a tight top on I wear a big loose shirt over it. I don't want to be ogled at by teenage boys, basically. That's quite a conscious decision that I have made." Her modest mode of dressing for school was a form of self-defense. It was a way of minimizing the extent to which she would be positioned as an object of sexual desire—spoken about, fantasized about, or harassed—by boy students.

A more extreme example of this was given by Nell Wilson (b. 1955), a teacher in a boys school, who found herself positioned as an object of the pornographic gaze of an unknown student who had inserted

> bits of pornographic material in my roll. The next thing was some women's underwear outside the classroom. The worst thing was two sheets of fairly graphic photographs of a woman baring all with a kid's writing all over it—he wrote me a kind of a love note that was quite obscene and shoved that in my classroom door. It was addressed to me.

Explicitly sexual images and language could be used by boys to exert power over women teachers. It could also be used to denigrate the bodies, and thereby to reject the ideas, of other women who entered their educational horizons, such as female poets or women characters in books. Nell Wilson had shown her class of senior boys a BBC (British Broadcasting Corporation) videotape that had been screened in New Zealand on a current events program, the *Fraser* show. This program had raised the problem of the widening gap between English boys' and girls' achievements in school—that girls were now outpacing boys:

> I had taped the *Fraser* program in which he had a panel discussion about why girls do better at school. I thought my seniors would be really interested in this because this is about kids their age and things they're going to have to face. And their reaction was really weird. As soon as I put it on, all they did was spend time trying to undermine the women on the program—saying, "She's got to be a lesbian, look at her, look at the clothes she's wearing! That person looks sick—they're feminists." They would not believe that I was showing it to them because I thought they might be interested in the consequences for them, if it was true. I hadn't expected that reaction at all. And yet I shouldn't have been surprised at all—the current term of abuse at Boys' High is to call each other "gay."

My reading of the boys' response is that they used homophobia to denigrate the bodies of the women in the video as a defense against their insecurities in the face of a threatened undermining of the boundaries of their binary construction of acceptable masculinity and acceptable femininity. This has also been observed in the international research literature (Mac An Ghaill, 1994; Trenchard & Warren, 1987; Youth Voices, 1996).

The permissive climate of the 1990s made it possible for students to use sexual terminology quite legitimately in the classroom. While in previous eras the topic of homosexuality could never have been raised in the classroom, there are today legitimate spaces in the curriculum for the discussion of such issues—not only in sexuality education itself, but also in mainstream subjects, such as English, since many great writers have been lesbian or—as was Foucault—gay (Miller, 1993; Sears, 1992a). The creation of legitimate spaces, however, can also offer students a new tool of resistance. Their use of the term *lesbian* (no longer a banned concept) as a term of abuse offered them a defense against "dangerous knowledge" that could have undermined the securities of the patriarchal gender order that they sought to preserve. Another example came from Veronica Neilson (b. 1969), who was also teaching in a boys school. She described how students used homophobic language in an attempt to regulate her appearance:

> Last year I had my hair cut really short like Anita McNaught's [a TV presenter], and one of the boys came up to me and said "Miss, you shouldn't have your hair cut like that because people are going to think you're a lesbian." And I said, "Oh, do you really think so?" And they said, "Yeah!" I said, "Oh well, if the shoe fits." I never tell them whether I am or whether I'm not.

This suggestion of homophobia as a grounds for the policing of teachers' dress is a theme which recurs throughout my data on the postreform era. Such surveillance by students and teachers of one another has been well documented in previous research (Khayatt, 1994; Quinlivan, 1996). As Carmen Luke and Jennifer Gore (1992b) have argued, "Women's sexualities—in their manifestation in dress, appearance/appeal, 'looks,' age, bodily habitus—continue to be read by many men as signposts of women's worth" (p. 201).

This so-called sexist male gaze can also be assumed by women in an attempt to regulate the compliance of other women to the norms of conventional femininity. Susan Godfrey (b. 1968) attended a teacher education program in the early 1990s. She was older than most of her classmates, had lived an "alternative lifestyle," and was now living with her baby and the child's father in a nuclear family situation. She had rejected the frills of feminine adornment: "My classmates were shying away from me because I had hairy legs and hairy armpits and short hair." Further examples of women applying such pressure were offered by Veronica Neilson, who commented that "women who don't have that [feminist] background are really trying to be something. We've got teachers at school who try to be bimbos and it's embarrassing." In a small-town coeducational school, Veronica's feminism had been challenged by the mothers of male students. She described such a challenge as resulting from one of her poetry lessons:

> There was one poem that talked about women's bodies being made to conform, and I was talking to the boys about what we see as beautiful and what we don't. And I had this very beautiful farmer's wife come in and ask me what I was trying to do—was I trying to make her son marry someone ugly or something? Another poem was about "the weight of the wedding band on Jennifer's hands." Talking about how men have often oppressed women. And I got backlash again.

While formal rules for teachers' dress have been relaxed, these women found themselves subjected to strong informal pressures—from students, from colleagues, and from parents—to conform to a conventional image of femininity which would leave intact a patriarchal, dualistic gender order.

With respect to the regulation of students' dress, most secondary schools have uniforms for at least the junior school (the early grades) although students often have considerable flexibility within the uniform requirements (for example, in the girls school that my daughter attended, girls may make their own summer dresses in any modest style from the regulation fabric). Most schools do not require uniforms for their senior students. Some of those interviewed had used their students' fascination with dress as curriculum material. Dress offered Julie King (b. 1969) a space to engage with her Pacific Islands students about feminist issues by meeting them on their own cultural ground. Discovering the influence of American music videos on the dress of her Pacific Island students, she made these a topic for feminist analysis in her English curriculum:

> On teaching practice [from college] I taught from music videos because I suddenly realized that the way the students were dressing—their hairstyles, the way they spoke, everything—was coming from the music videos in American films. They all wanted to be gangstas. I stopped the video every 10 seconds and we analysed what kind of image it was—whether it was a male image, a female one, a dance one or whatever—and the boys seemed totally oblivious to the fact that they were predominantly male images that we were seeing . . . .When I started my first job in this

school, which has no uniform, the kids were actually wearing the stuff. Their hairstyles were from music videos and the way they talked with their body with all this rap gangsta kind of stuff.

The covert regulation of students' dress in those schools that have abolished uniforms would make a fruitful area of future inquiry. Such schools retain the powers to monitor and regulate students' clothing by means of a dress code. For example, one such school's present dress code reads:

> In keeping with this school's emphasis on self-management, there are no uniform regulations. The development of sensible attitudes towards matters of dress and appearance is seen as part of the educational process and students are asked to avoid extravagance of style or appearance . . . . In any question of acceptability of dress the school's decision will be final.

In practice, such dress codes can result in a covert normalizing process whereby those students whose adolescent struggles are manifested in an extravagance of style, such as seen in the case of punks and avant-garde youth, are excluded or expelled from the school. *Sensible* means average. While in previous eras, teachers' and students' dress was more overtly regulated through formal dress codes and uniforms, the mid-1990s are characterized by more informal micropractices of power which inscribe on the bodies of teachers and students the values of the wider society.

Body-Spaces

"Discipline," wrote Foucault (1977), "proceeds from the distribution of bodies in space" (p. 141). As the next chapter will illustrate, there were, in my data concerning the present, legacies—traces—of past regimes of truth with respect to the sexual segregations and command of space. Here I shall mention two—some questions concerning coeducation, and issues concerning some boys' resistances to movement in "progressive" classroom activities. Many of the older men who were interviewed had themselves attended all-boys schools and, although some of them had taught in such single-sex institutions, they said that the all-male cultures of these needed "softening" through the presence of female teachers and pupils. Such views were concisely summarized by George Reed (b. 1926):

> I didn't like caning. I didn't like bullying. I didn't like boys on their own; I thought they needed some girls to sort of soften the edges. I enjoyed the company of men. I enjoyed the staff room in

single sex schools, and yet I also enjoyed the staff room at coeducational.

David Don (b. 1932) had taught long-term in a boys school and although he "couldn't get [female pupils] in the senior school," he had worked hard at convincing the principal that, "women could contribute a great deal to the school. They have been on the staff ever since and some of the women colleagues that I taught with were superb. They would lend a different aspect to things. Yet they got a lot of resistance from some people." This enthusiasm for having women staff in boys schools was widespread among many of the men who had worked in such schools.

Many of the women said that they enjoyed teaching boys both in coeducational and single-sex environments. However, as shown earlier, some of the younger women mentioned that they sometimes felt uncomfortable under the sexualizing gaze of male adolescents and had experienced harassment of various sorts (Lees, 1993; Linn, Stein, Young, & Davis, 1992). Others had experienced discrimination in terms of employment advancement opportunities. To help them deal with such experiences, a number of the women had become involved in the organization of women teachers groups in boys schools or in coeducational settings. Sometimes this was regarded with suspicion, even hostility, by male colleagues. For example, Sian Murray (b. 1963) had become the women's officer for her branch of the New Zealand Post-Primary Teachers' Association, or NZPPTA (a teachers union) in a coeducational school in a conservative region of New Zealand:

> I had to organise women's meetings, which was really good for all
> the staff. We used to have a lot of women's dinners. The men
> didn't like that, but we still had them anyway. And then the re-
> gional women's officer used to come down and have seminars,
> and so I would organise those. The chairperson at that time was a
> female, so she was really supportive.

During the 1980s a number of state and private boys schools had opened their door to senior girls from other schools (Rout, 1992). This had the effect of "creaming off" some of the more able girls from the senior classes in the neighboring girls schools. Eric Cotton (b. 1939) was the principal of a boys school, which, together with the local girls school, had set up a senior college that involved his seventh-form (senior) boys going to the nearby girls school for certain subjects and the seventh-form girls coming to his school for others. He was aware that his well-resourced school had better facilities than those at the girls school:

[When I started working at a boys school] I missed the girls, because they do soften the place. But they love coming here because
it's nicer than their place to be in; and they really appreciate that.
And I think it's ideal. I don't think I would have been happy staying on here with just boys. No, I like girls.

In his interview, he offered a thoughtful analysis on the relative benefits of
single-sex education and coeducation for boys and for girls at different
stages of their adolescent development. He believed that in early adolescence girls were more powerful than boys and that the self-esteem of boys
was best nurtured in these junior years in single-sex settings. For example,
some girls used their superior verbal skills to put boys down in a way that
was damaging to the boys' self-esteem when they were in the early stages of
adolescence and less mature physically, intellectually, and emotionally than
were the girls:

I'm convinced that boys do well at third, fourth, and fifth form in
single-sex boys schools. The girls aren't there to put them down.
Put-downs are the worst things that happen at schools—that's the
type of bullying when there's the name-calling, not the physical
stuff. Girls are better motivated at 13, 14, 15, they're neater,
they're tidier, they're more aware of what they need to do. And
the boys are ugly. They become semi-ugly at about 15 or 16, and
then they become human. And girls at 13 or 14, if they're powerful, are looking at guys 15 or 16; they're looking at the guys who
are decent, they're not looking at these guys who are the same
age. They're ahead of them. They know more about themselves,
and about the boys, than the boys know about them. They think
a lot more. They talk a lot more. The boys are out there doing
things, and yelling and screaming and swearing and things. And
so, what I've noticed here [at a boys school] is that they work a
lot harder. And you can really crank into them, because boys are
pretty simple creatures. It's not running them down, but you
know, you can say something simply to a boy and he'll probably
accept it. Whereas with girls, they'll want to argue the finer details because they're more intelligent or more aware at a younger
age, of themselves. But I think single-sex schooling is ludicrous at
16 or 17 when the boys have caught up and the girls are good
too. No one talks about senior kids in disparaging terms, they always worry about the 13-, 14-, 15-year-olds; that's where the
problems are.

Another example of boys' being damaged by put-downs was given by Rangi Davidson (b. 1956), who—in an analysis reminiscent of that of Paul Willis (1977)—was concerned that so many working-class Maori boys rejected intellectual work as being the province of "nerds" and therefore as being "unmanly." He did not say whether it was girls or other boys who were applying the nerd label to the working-class, academically successful Maori boys whom he taught, but explained that (Maori and Pakeha) girls did not experience the same pressures, because academic success was more acceptable in their peer group culture (see also Carkeek, Davies, & Irwin, 1994):

> Girls are better learners. They work harder. They get on with the job. But when they have a bad day, wow, watch out! Whereas boys tend to be more aloof, tough-boy images come through a lot. They don't show their emotions as much, which is the tough-boy image again. But they don't work as well as girls. They are frightened to show that they work hard. It's a lot to do with peer pressure. I know the intelligent Maori boys at our school [in a small town with a high Maori population], they get the nerd label or whatever you want to call it.

While Rangi cast this resistance as being a characteristic of working-class Maori boys, Nell Wilson (b. 1955) had similar difficulties in her English class in a boys school with a predominantly Pakeha and largely middle-class student population. As a student-centered teacher, she wanted her students to work in groups, to initiate inquiries, and to engage in debates on controversial issues. She wanted a classroom with flexible use of space, freedom of movement, and interaction between students as a basis for learning. Instead, she found that the boys, accustomed to a static environment—formal and examination oriented—resisted her pedagogic style; the boys demanded that they sit still while she fed them notes:

> It was a real struggle there. I just couldn't believe how it was. All the boys wanted was, "Look, if you give us the notes, we'll have the right answers." That's all they were interested in. They didn't want to talk about anything, they just wanted the right answers. . . . The boys have been just so resistant to getting out of their chairs, for one thing, and talking to each other, for another, and actually sharing information. They seem like they don't want to do that at all. So I don't know whether it's a boys' thing or just a Boys' High thing.

It seems that it is the ethos of a particular community of students, structured by the traditions and micropractices of a particular school over time—whether single-sex or coeducational—that creates the climate of the classrooms, in which the constraints on and possibilities for teachers' pedagogies are constructed.

Managing Behavior

I conclude with a brief discussion of the normalization of students' behavior in the late 1990s. The example that I have chosen comes from a boys school. Since the abolition of corporal punishment, nonviolent forms of discipline have been required. By the late 1980s, prepackaged systems for behavior management were being disseminated and marketed to the boards of trustees, who now have the powers to acquire such packages. Often of American origin, these packages are frequently based on the humanistic and behavioral psychologies. Assertive discipline programs (based on behaviorist premises) have been marketed to schools by the SES (Special Education Services) and some of the younger teachers I interviewed spoke favourably of the sense of structure these provided them with. Several schools have introduced a peer support program as an alternative to corporal punishment. While the older regimes of discipline rested on students' fear of overt methods of punishment, these contemporary ones rely on the panoptic gaze of both teachers and students—a relation of surveillance:

> The peer support system is a superb thing. We've got 50 kids this year who are sixth formers [seniors] who have volunteered to work with our third formers [juniors] next year. They were all here on the new entrants day last week when we had all the next year's third formers here. They were showing them what to do. Working with them. In the exams and the tests with them. All this sort of thing, so you're taking a vertical system and leveling it out a fair bit. Working with the prefects to make sure that there's no nastiness, nothing that's at all awkward. . . . What we've done here is to set up a climate in the school where we've got an agreement with the kids that certain things won't happen. When you go around the school you see in every classroom the class climate. We stress "three C's": Courtesy, Cooperation, Common sense; keeping things very, very simple. No yelling and screaming at people; no thumping them. We've got rid of teachers who are physical. We get a lot of little boys around the school who are safe. I keep asking them. I ask people to ask them. I show a lot of people around the school while it's working . . . . And every time I do

that I find that it's good. No organized fights. There used to be organized fights every year. It's been very important to us to make sure that the kids are feeling good at the place.

While removing the physical violence, the spectacle, and the fear associated with corporal punishment, the covert modes of regulation of behavior retain certain features that were identified by Foucault as characteristic of the capillary workings of modern power. As in the case of prefects administering punishment on behalf of teachers (by the cane or by confinements such as detention), peer support rests on the recruitment of students as "agents" for the teachers. As Foucault observed about previous eras, in some contemporary school disciplinary practices "pupils were selected to act as 'officers' whose task it was to observe the others and report all cases of bad behaviour" (Sheridan, 1980, p. 153). Although such elaborate systems of surveillance are not new in schools, what may be new is the reliance on students of the same age to monitor the behavior of their peers.

DISCUSSION

What discourses are enacted in the disciplinary practices described in these accounts? Competing discourses on questions of sexual identity, sexual orientation, and appropriate demeanors for women and for men are evident in these stories. They do not speak of a monolithic New Right hegemony or of a homogenizing patriarchy, although traces of class, racial, colonial, patriarchal, and heterosexist power relations are present. Rather, they offer glimpses of the workings of multiple, changing, simultaneous, and contradictory relations of power. As previous ethnographies have shown, individuals are variously and multiply positioned in schools—at times powerful and at others less so—in relation to others (e.g., Connell et al., 1982; A. Jones, 1991; Kenway, Willis, Blackmore, & Rennie, 1993; Walkerdine, 1987). Through Foucauldian lenses, power indeed shows up as "capillary," as it flows through all parts of the school's "corporate body." All individuals channel power: Students and teachers police each others' outward appearance, deportment, and behavior, although it is the teacher who officially has power over the students.

These stories offer many examples of the surveillance and regulating— by female and male students, teachers, and parents—of "conventional" (patriarchal) heterosexuality. For example, the "official" (legislative) discourse concerning sexual orientation is libertarian, and this gave permission for students and teachers to talk about homosexuality. However, homophobia was evident in some female and male students' surveillance of one another and of their teachers: "She's got to be a lesbian . . . look at the clothes she's wearing"; and "the current term of abuse at Boys' High is call each other 'gay'" (Khyatt, 1994; Quinlivan, 1996).

Younger women who taught teenage boys were sensitive to the allure of their own bodies as objects of the boys' heterosexual erotic fantasies and, accordingly, covered themselves: "I don't wear tight clothes. . . . I don't want to be ogled at by teenage boys, basically." In this case the boys were of Pacific Islands origin, and modesty of dress is important in many of New Zealand's Pacific Island Christian communities; this may have influenced this teacher's adoption of the dress of a "good, modest woman." There are other suggestions in the data that women and girls were dichotomized according to the sexual double standard as "good women" and "whores" (with feminists being associated with whores). As Walkerdine's (1987) research has shown, male students who position woman teachers as mere "fuckable objects" reverse the official balance of power between adult (teacher) over child (student): There were "bits of pornographic material in my roll. . . . [A kid] wrote me a kind of love note that was quite obscene." Here the discourse of sexist pornography offers male students the power of consumers—a highly valorized position in the "busnocratic rationality" (Peters & Marshall, 1996) of New Right discourses. This will be explored further in Chapter Four.

There are also resistances and oppositions—by men and women—to dominant discourses concerning masculinity and femininity: "There are no relations of power without resistances; the latter are all the more real and effective because they are formed right at the point where relations of power are exercised" (Foucault, 1980b, p. 142). A women's discourse of resistance is feminism (see Chapter Three). However, as others have found in research (Kenway et al., 1993), some students and teachers conceptualize feminists as being pathological—whores, ugly, unfeminine, and lesbian—used, of course, in a perjorative sense: "That person looks sick—they're feminists," and "My classmates were shying away from me because I had hairy legs and long hair" (Khyatt, 1994; Quinlivan, 1996; Trudell, 1992). There was an account of female teachers who were seen by their feminist colleague as resisting the feminist stereotype through trying "to be bimbos." Some students used their pathologization of feminists as a justification for resisting information that threatened the binary distinctions (or boundaries) of the patriarchal gender order that they sought to preserve (Connell et al., 1982), such as recent statistics that showed girls out-performing boys (McDonald, 1992; Sturrock, 1993) or "a poem about the weight of the wedding band on Jennifer's hands . . . I got backlash again." There was an account of male staff members who opposed the desire of their feminist colleagues to spend time discussing women's concerns at their union's "women's dinners. The men didn't like that."

The pathologization of feminists (and feminisms) is a current center of interest for a number of feminist researchers. Some of these have drawn on Julia Kristeva's (1986) psychoanalytic notion of "the abject" in helping them to understand some people's abhorrence of feminists as dirty, polluting, and violating of distinctions between the inside and outside of pure categories (Butler, 1993; Watson, 1996)—a view behind arguments that others have applied to practices of ethnic segregations and desegregations (or "multiculturalism") (Sibley, 1995).

Resistances to some of the harsher conventions of macho masculinity were also evident from some of the men. An ambivalence toward coeducation was a striking example. Several male teachers disliked the all-male cultures in single-sex schools and thought that boys needed women teachers and girls "to soften the edges." Conversely, though, the presence of girls could be hurtful to some boys in the younger age groups. Girls' earlier physical maturity (a discourse of human development) was given as a reason. With their superior verbal skills, girls were capable of "the type of bullying where there's the name-calling." Single-sex schooling was seen by some as protection for younger boys, who were perceived as being less powerful and successful than were girls in the vulnerable years of these boys' early teens.

It is useful to conceptualize disciplining sexuality within the parameters of the discipline of the body and control of the population more broadly, for—as later chapters will elaborate—threaded through these narratives are stories about the intertwined inequalities between classes and races—traces of capitalist/colonial relations (Bhabha, 1994; Said, 1993). The discourse of managerialism shines through in one account of the school in a community in which the parents were predominantly in professional/managerial occupations: "the clothes [were] very bold, black and white . . . the staff were into power dressing." Conversely, there were the working-class "Maori boys: frightened to show that they work hard . . . they get the nerd label." Global multinational capitalist relations and cultural imperialism show through: "The way the [Pacific Island] kids were dressing—their hairstyles, the way they spoke, everything—was coming from the music videos in American films. They all wanted to be gangstas." American prepackaged programs—based on humanistic and behavioral psychologies—were purchased and used for the surveillance and behavioral control of students and in pedagogic practice. My contrapuntal reading reveals, then, both "the metropolitan history that is narrated and . . . those other histories against which (and together with which) the dominating discourse acts" (Said, 1993, p. 59).

These stories about disciplining sexuality in the schools of the 1990s usefully clothe Foucault's conceptual framework. As Chris Weedon (1987) has pointed out, "not all discourses . . . carry equal weight or power" (p.

35). By dramatizing dominant and subordinate discourses, they offer a three-dimensional view of theories in action. When the stories of real people are positioned *inside* the educational and wider social theories that we study in university courses, they offer an alternative to textbook presentations of these theories as typologies or flat maps. The discursive field of educational ideas of a time and place is, as Dorothy Smith (1987) puts it, "like a conversation mediated by texts that is not a matter of statements alone but of actual ongoing practices and sites of practices" (p. 214).

CHAPTER TWO

Time Travels:
Canes, Berets, and Rock n Roll

I argued in Chapter One that the theories, policies, and practices of present-day schooling are premised on both the ideal of freedom and the necessity for social control. It is this apparent contradiction, said Foucault, that is productive of human endeavours in the interwoven dimensions of social (including educational) theorizing, policymaking and its implementation, and everyday teaching and other professional practices:

> I believe that the process which has really rendered the discourse of the human sciences possible is the juxtaposition, the encounter between two lines of approach, two mechanisms, two absolutely heterogeneous types of discourse: on the one hand there is the re-organisation of right that invests sovereignty, and on the other, the mechanics of the coercive forces whose exercise takes a disciplinary form. (Foucault, 1980b, p. 107)

I shall explore further the lived realities of this tension in education by traveling back to the secondary schools of the 1920s, which is as far as the living memories of my interviewees permit me, then work my way up through the strata of time as revealed by the excavations of my database. I shall close this history of the present at the point where the last chapter began—the mid-1980s.

As in other Western countries, New Zealand's educational writers (historians and policymakers) have drawn conceptual maps of the shifts in the discourses concerning the "right that invests sovereignty" that have shaped government policies for public schools (Beeby, 1986; Renwick, 1986). Although the details of these categorizations have varied with respect to secondary schools in the twentieth century, these writers have identified certain core values and ideas as characterizing four or five distinct phases or stages in New Zealand's educational development. Although I question the teleological implications of such maps, they provide me with a useful starting point for constructing a framework with which to explore the discipline of the (sexual) body in intermediate and secondary schools recalled from living memory.

According to Beeby (1986) and Renwick (1986), government policies on schooling in the early twentieth century — the first phase — were based on social Darwinist notions of the survival of the fittest. While this idea continued into the 1920s and 1930s, it was modified during the second phase by an increasing — and psychologically informed — emphasis on the developmental needs of the individual child. The third phase is the post–World War II era, a time that has been described by many writers as having been shaped by the government's prioritizing of a social-democratic version of equality of opportunity that was premised on the notion that equal means the same. The fourth phase is the period from the late 1960s to the early 1980s, when there was an increasing focus on pluralism, diversity, and freedom of student choice. While historians have not yet explored in any depth the period since the mid-1980s when restructuring began, sociologists and others have added a fifth set of discourses that have dominated the policies of this era (Codd, Harker, & Nash, 1990; Lauder & Wylie, 1990; Middleton, Codd, & Jones, 1990). These writers have identified a fifth regime of truth which is characterized by a dual (and contradictory) emphasis on New Right economic assumptions and on targeting to achieve equality of outcomes — the *present* that was outlined in the previous chapter.

When I began this cross-sectional analysis of my interview data, I tried to squeeze it into this chronological framework. However, the men who mapped the eras did not explore whether these divisions signified changes in the ways sexuality was conceptualized by policymakers or discursively constructed in schools. I was curious to see whether the shifts in the discursive construction of sex and gender relations[1] that had been identified in feminist studies (Fry, 1985; O'Neill, 1992; Tennant, 1986) corresponded with the eras identified in the general history texts. A policymaker's perspective is a view from the top — as the overarching perspective of the manpower planner, it explains the ideals, reviews the relevant information, and articulates the strategies by means of which schooling is intended to regulate and shape the population. However, when viewed from the bottom up, the disciplinary practices described by my informants — those which regulated their embodied sexuality — refused to fit neatly into the top-down categorizations of the government policymakers. These stories from teachers about everyday life in the schools that they had attended as pupils and in those in which they taught, reveal assumptions and practices which were often out of step with the rationalist ideals of the state. While there is some relationship between such practices and the broader "myths" (Beeby, 1986) or eras identified by the historians and policymakers, my data suggest that disciplinary practices characteristic of former eras continued unchanged in specific schools contemporaneously with newer forms of discipline and educational thinking, and the data reveal continuities as well as change.

My approach, then, in the following analysis, will be both chronological and thematic. Each cross section, or slice, of chronological time is viewed from the perspectives found in the memories of multiple generations — of those who were children, adolescents, and adults of the time. This enables me to focus on ways in which the bodily disciplining of teachers and their students are interdependent. For, as Sari Biklen (1995) explained, "school rules regulate both students and teachers. Teachers' bodies are regulated by the very restrictions they establish for the children . . . adults' days [are] controlled by needing to be placed in a supervisory position in relation to children" (p. 179). On occasions the slice-of-time approach is blurred, for when my data raise a theme in one era and some informants carry this theme through into later segments of chronological time, I have (as in the case of the material on caning) run with the theme rather than with the chronology.

DISCIPLINING THE STUDENT BODY: FROM THE 1920s TO 1945

In New Zealand, from the late nineteenth century through the 1920s — as in Britain (D. Jones, 1990; Walkowitz, 1980) and the United States (Davis, 1981) — Social Darwinist ideas about how to ensure the survival of the fittest underpinned a highly selective secondary school system. With their predominantly British academic curricula, New Zealand's public and private secondary schools were intended for an academic and professional elite. From 1920–1935 this discourse was augmented by the influence of progressivism, as the new international psychological and psychoanalytic movements in child development gained influence in local contexts (May, 1992a). Although this chapter is concerned with secondary schools, it is important to point out that in the early to middle years of the twentieth century the progressive, or child-centered, influences became highly influential, and eventually dominant, in early childhood and infant school education and that it was the improvizations of ordinary classroom teachers rather than, or as much as, the dictates of policymakers that underpinned this phenomenon (May, 1992a; Middleton, 1996c, 1996d; Middleton & May, 1997). As Foucault (1980b) expressed it, "in order for there to be a movement from above to below there has to be a capillarity from below to above at the same time" (p. 201).

During the 1920s and into the 1930s, Freudian psychological and psychoanalytic theories of child development were increasingly allied with technologies such as the intelligence test (Olssen, 1988; Walkerdine, 1984) and made it possible for educators to focus more specifically on the perceived "needs" of the individual, although this continued to be done within the parameters of a highly selective and differentiated secondary school system. Under the leadership of the director of education George Hogben, the availability of secondary schooling was extended by the provision of technical high schools for those who were perceived as being less academic or who chose a vocationally based education and training for the new industries and offices which were being established (Day, 1992). During these years junior high schools were also introduced at least in part as a means of identifying the kind of secondary school, academic or technical, for which a child was "best fitted"—genetically, intellectually, or psychologically (Openshaw, Lee, & Lee, 1993).

While many historians have studied the ways in which social Darwinism supported the retention of class and racial hierarchies on the grounds that these were "natural" (McGeorge, 1981; McKenzie, 1975), feminists have pointed out that, in addition, the social Darwinist and individual needs theories of the first third of the twentieth century were premised on strict prescriptions for the differentiated disciplining of male and female bodies in the family and the school (Fry, 1985; Olssen, 1981; Tennant, 1986). Despite the protestations of some key women doctors and feminist teachers of the time (Bunkle, 1980b; Tennant, 1986), the weight of medical and popular opinion supported schooling and child-rearing practices that emphasised a Spartan bodily discipline, including military training, for boys, and a watered-down academic curriculum, which would include compulsory domestic science in the place of higher mathematics and physics, for girls (Fry, 1985; Olssen, 1981; Tennant, 1986). As in Britain, Europe, and North America (D. Jones, 1990), medical science in New Zealand conceptualized the human body as having only a fixed amount of energy, and many scientists argued that too much cram could damage the bodies of both sexes.

The discovery of child sexuality by doctors and psychoanalysts produced guidelines for parents on how to prevent social pathology in children, and thereby in the wider society. They must monitor the most intimate of their children's bodily habits; the feeding and bowel movements of babies were to be regulated by the clock; and "vices" such as "infantile onanism" (masturbation) and homosexuality were to be prevented or medically—even surgically—treated (Olssen, 1981; Parkinson, 1991). The Victorian age, argued Foucault (1980a), had been conventionally portrayed as being repressive of sexuality. However, it could equally be described as being *productive*—of hundreds of medical texts, religious tracts, and policing behaviours in clinics, families, hospitals, and schools: "Rather than a massive censorship, beginning with the verbal proprieties imposed by the Age of Reason, what was involved was a regulated and polymorphous incitement to discourse" (p. 43). He argued that within schools,

> what one might call the internal discourse of the institution—the one it employed to address itself, and which circulated among those who made it function—was largely based on this assumption that this sexuality existed, that it was precocious, active, and ever present. (p. 28)

Throughout the Western world, the dominant medical and other scientific theories of the early twentieth century—social Darwinism, eugenics, and "vital energies" theories—supported a differentiated secondary schooling for boys and girls (Davis, 1981; Fry, 1985; Tolerton, 1992; Tennant, 1986; Walkowitz, 1985). Erik Olssen illustrates the ideal with the help of quotations from the works of Sir Truby King:

> Boys needed "a cold bath in the morning . . . plenty of open-air exercise . . . and very little evening work"; girls, endangered by "over-exertion," often ended up in mental asylums. Worse, over-exertion at academic work impaired "the potentialities of reproduction and healthy maternity." . . . If girls worked too hard at school they would become, as King liked to say, citing Herbert Spencer as his authority, flat-chested and unfitted for maternity. Educating women for domesticity, he believed, would give "an enormous benefit to the women, and prospectively to the race." (Olssen, 1981, p. 11)

King was no isolated eccentric. A product of the influential Edinburgh Medical School, he was the founder of New Zealand's Plunket Society—the organization that employed nurses to visit homes and monitor women's mothering skills and the health of their babies: "By 1930 some 65% of all non-Maori infants were under the control and care of the Society; by 1947 the figure had risen to 85%" (p. 11). King was one of the leading opponents of an advanced secondary school academic education for girls, arguing on medical grounds that this—and in particular the study of advanced mathematics and physical sciences—could weaken women's physiological capacities for menstruation and reproduction. This view also tied up with eugenicist notions—that it was women's responsibility to breed a healthy, British, "race" and men's to defend it (Tennant, 1986; Olssen, 1981; Tolerton, 1992). A schooling that would center on women's "natural role," to be wives and mothers, was justified by these "scientific" beliefs in a strong "link between scientific racism, degeneracy and the empire" (Walkerdine, 1984, p. 173).

New Zealand was one of the later British colonies, its constitutional foundation dating from 1840, when the Treaty of Waitangi was signed by British officials and Maori chiefs (Orange, 1989). According to social Darwinists, New Zealand's indigenous Maori were higher up in the evolutionary scale of races than were African peoples or Australian Aborigines, and school geography and civics textbooks reflected and reiterated this belief (McGeorge, 1981). New Zealanders were not subjected to miscegenation laws—as were settlers in some North American and African colonies (Bhabha, 1994; Davis, 1981), and intermarriage between Maori and Pakeha, or white settlers, was common and remains so (Eldred-Grigg, 1984; Papakura, 1983).

In the early days of contact, many Maori were keen to become literate, to attend schools, and to set up trading and business relationships with white settlers. However, by the late nineteenth century the early trickle of settlers had swelled to an invasion; much Maori land was alienated from them through trickery; wars were fought; and *mana* (power, prestige, reputation) was low. Thousands died from imported diseases to which they had no immunity, and Maori were said to be a dying but noble race (Barrington & Beaglehole, 1974; McGeorge, 1981; Openshaw, Lee, & Lee, 1993). When a national system of public primary schools was established in 1877 under a central department of education, most Maori children were living in remote rural areas and many attended separate Native schools.[2] The emphasis on health in these schools also had implications for the students' sexuality. The primary schooling of Maori boys was oriented towards farming, whereas Maori girls would be schooled as the future wives of farmers and taught the appropriate European domestic skills:

> The boys—they had about an acre of ground out there that they
> dug up and put into vegetables and things, and they all got the
> vegetables to take home. They were very proud of that. They
> learned a lot of practical things, those kids, about how to manage
> themselves and how to run their households when they grew up.

The conceptual framework in which the education of Maori was envisioned was part of the broader British imperialist strategy: The proper disciplining of white boys and girls in school would ensure the continued military and moral strength of the British Empire and the subjugation of "colored" races (Bhabha, 1994; Davis, 1981; Said, 1993). New Zealand's Maori were seen as intelligent, "civilizable," and capable of being educated towards eventual equality. However, apart from a small academic and professional elite who attended the church-run Maori boarding schools, few Maori adolescents attended secondary schools in the early years of the century (Openshaw, Lee, & Lee, 1993). Because I have so little data on

Maori in secondary schools before 1945, I offer as illustration the following brief excerpts concerning primary schools.

The interpenetrations of the disciplinary apparatuses for health, education, and welfare were particularly evident in accounts by Maori pupils and their teachers. One teacher in a rural Native School recalled: "We used to have head inspections for nits and *kutu* [head lice]. We had to doctor all their sores. We had to give them cod-liver oil. The District Nurse [public health nurse] came in once a week or oftener if required." Distinctions between Maori and non-Maori were reinforced by such well-meant practices, the administration of which made Maori children in mixed schools stand out when they were required to "Stand!" or to "remain after class" or morning assembly to see the visiting public health nurse. In order for policies on Maori health and education to be formulated, statistics on Maori schoolchildren were required by the state authorities. One teacher in a rural school remembered the difficulties of identifying Maori children by "blood" (rather than by using today's concept of identity according to one's chosen cultural affiliation) when filling in the required forms for the education authorities:

> Once during the year you had to put in a Return [form] on the
> Maori children and those who were half [termed *half-castes* at the
> time]. I said to a girl called Hine, "You must be half." "No."
> "Now, your mother is white?" "Yes." "Well then, you're half."
> "No." I said, "If your mother is white and your father is a Maori,
> that's half and half." "No." I said, "Why not?" "My grandfather
> [father's mother] is one-eighth Spanish." Which, accordingly,
> made her fifteen thirty-seconds. But she wasn't sixteen thirty-
> seconds [half] and she didn't want to be. And she was quite right.

My Pakeha informants' stories about junior high school and secondary schooling in the 1920s and 1930s told of micropractices that were consistent with the social goals of the "domestication" of women and the "toughening" of men. To illustrate these, I trace two of the themes which recurred in my interviews about this period: physical punishment and coeducation.

Consistent with the ethos of toughening boys, the carefully controlled administering of the cane by male teachers was common. Foucault (1977) described the physical chastisement of the body as the method of punishment characteristic of preindustrial eras in which the spectacle of the ritual played as large a part in maintaining order as did the physical act itself. While the secondary schools of the 1920s and 1930s in other ways epitomized the rationalized, administrative approach to discipline characteristic of the modern age, the ritual administrations of corporal punishment—as observed in previous research (Mercurio, 1972)—can be understood as a residue, an archaeological trace, of a premodern past. As Paul Patton (1979) has written, "Under the old regime, where punishment itself was a spectacle, the focus was not so much on the criminal but on the crime itself and the instances of power charged with its expiation" (p. 132).

This was graphically described by Barry Keith (b. 1931), who had attended a prestigious state boys school in a city as recently as the 1950s:

> I remember the first day because my form master really terrified me. The first thing he did was to show us the range of canes that he had. He had this box alongside his desk and he held up canes of different lengths and thicknesses and informed us how the canes were to be graded. The bigger you got, the heavier the cane. I remember that very well.

In a few boys schools this tradition continued unbroken right into the late 1980s, when corporal punishment was outlawed. For example, Nigel Howard (b. 1970) described the ways in which the boys at a provincial boys high school regarded their abilities to withstand the pain of being caned as a source of pride and prestige:

> He got marched out with the teacher's hand around his collar and down to the caning room. I've looked in the caning room—you go into this small room, and there's just canes right around the walls. They had to have another teacher there as a witness; they had to sign their name in the book, and that sort of thing. And then the guys would come back with a notch in the belt. And your *mana* would be in terms of how many notches you had in your belt.

A somewhat different, romanticized view of the place of corporal punishment in the making of a man—reminiscent of the English public school ethos—was that offered by Raymond Wilson (b. 1939). The idea of taking your punishment like a man was integral to the chivalric code of honor that he had imbibed through "the role model thing" and his reading of English books for boys from the age of 7 or 8: "*Boys' Own* magazines—the hero figures in them. *Teddy Lester's School Days*. *William* books. Anything to do with sport. . . . I can remember in the third form [junior year] reading *The White Company* and the Conan Doyle ones." Isolated for a substantial part of his time from women, he developed an idealized view of the female sex as being up on a pedestal and mentioned reading about "The Code of Chivalry, and the Knights in Shining Armour going off and rescuing the damsel in distress, those kind of romantic chivalrous tales." When, in 1953, he went to a metropolitan boys school, he found a culture which was continuous with his boyhood fantasies and in which team sports were central to the formation of a romantic image of masculinity:

> I can remember particularly when I was a boy the code of honor:
> that if you were naughty and you got caught you took your pun-
> ishment like a man, even though it hurt. You wouldn't ever
> sneak, and you wouldn't let somebody else take the blame. . . .
> You didn't tell lies. You owned up and took your punishment.
> The grammar school was an extension of what I'd been reading
> about. You came in as a snotty-nosed third former, and you saw
> the giants of men in the seventh form. They played for the first
> eleven in cricket, and the first fifteen in rugby. They were Gods,
> and you admired them. And when you heard something not to
> their credit you didn't know what to make of it, because the foun-
> dations of your world were being shaken. There was a good deal
> of romance in it.

While this man's experiences in an all-boys school had been pleasurable and benign, one or two of the other men had attended boys schools in which bullying was not only tolerated but encouraged, through the use of prefects who caned other students. For example, David Don (b. 1932) said that "Prefects used to cane, which I think is outrageous. Very early in my teaching career I was opposed to corporal punishment of any sort. But even the prefects did it." As a beginning teacher in the 1950s, he had to use the cane in order to survive. His small stature made him vulnerable in a setting in which size and authority were correlated:

> To start with you were just part of the system. I was just a begin-
> ning teacher. You're not able to challenge the whole thing, so you
> become part of it. I used the cane, but I don't think I could have
> been very much feared because I wasn't that strong physical type.
> But then fairly early on I decided it was a very bad thing.

A similar perspective was outlined by George Reed (b. 1926). When he took up a position as a senior house master in a state boys boarding school in the early 1960s, he found that a system of institutionalised physical punishment was deeply inscribed in the culture of the dormitory. Physical violence went deeper than the ritual administrations of the cane in formal settings (Mercurio, 1972), and the culture of the boarding part of the school had become centered around an acceptance of bullying, to which the school authorities turned a blind eye:

> Being the senior house master was a memorable time. There were 280 boys; bullying was rampant, and respected. I was in charge of these 280 boys. I had house masters under me. My main task as far as I was concerned was to get rid of bullying, which I did with some success, never fully. It was right in the grain of the school. Before my time somebody was roasted over the fire, that sort of thing. After I left, fortunately not when I was there, they threatened to hang a boy, and they put him on a chair. And they said, If you don't do something or other, we'll hang you. And he got scared and jumped.

At first it may seem that the use of physical force in boys schools may have little, if any, relevance to the lives and perspectives of women teachers, apart from the few who taught in boys schools. However, the constraints and possibilities of the work of women teachers are always and already inscribed by the wider social order. Women's competence to handle male students beyond the early primary school years has been questioned throughout the history of schooling because of their perceived lack of physical strength and stature and has been used as a rationale to confine women teachers to the junior classes (May, 1992a; Grumet, 1988). Sari Biklen (1995) posed the question, "Could women 'manage' larger boys" (p. 179)? Peter Harris (b. 1907) described how, in his early primary school teaching career in the 1920s, girls and boys received different punishments for the same "offense" (making mistakes in their school work):

> The cane was used when I first started, and shortly afterwards they brought in the strap, but not for girls. You just had to talk to them, perhaps give them some other form of punishment. I didn't have any difficulty. I think the way you handled them was the main thing. Children got punished for their work in those days. Used to get punished for not knowing a spelling, or for very little, with harsh punishment. Not all used it.

Several of those interviewed—both women and men—reported having been beaten by women teachers. Paul Barton (b. 1936) had attended a small-town secondary school between 1950–1951 and had been put off French by a brutal woman teacher:

> I had the most incredibly tyrannical French teacher who used to beat the hell out of anybody who made any mistake—you got

belted for every mistake you made in your French vocabulary. So
there was always this lineup of kids at the end of the period who
got whacked by this teacher.

Some of the women teachers whom I interviewed found their authority
challenged by boys and, in order to survive in the job, found it necessary to
resort to the use of corporal punishment. For example, Vera Grant (b.
1929) explained her initial difficulties in a new coeducational high school
in the early 1960s:

> I had a 4M—a technical class—for full maths. In those days, if
> you wanted to do an apprenticeship you had to do full maths.
> They'd put me in it deliberately because nobody else could cope
> with them. And I couldn't, either. I'd never, ever, had a boy
> strapped in my life, and one boy was giving me absolute hell. I'd
> had enough, and I sent him out to get strapped. And it's very inter-
> esting—I didn't entirely agree with the anti–corporal punishment
> campaigners on these things because of that incident. That boy
> walked back, walked into the class, beamed at me, sat down, and
> said, "Shut up, you fellows, and listen to the teacher!" and I
> didn't have any problems with the class. He respected me, he re-
> ally did. I think it was the principal that you sent them to in those
> days . . . . That was a lesson to me, that there are different peo-
> ple who react to different types of discipline. I had an enormous
> influence on that boy, and he still beams at me if he sees me in the
> street.

Conversely, some men reported difficulties in controlling the classroom
behavior of girls in coeducational settings. For example, Ernest McKenzie
(b. 1928) described a disagreement about this issue in 1950 between students at teachers college (many of whom were assertive returned servicemen)[3] and their aging and authoritarian lecturer:

> One of the "old digs" (the returned men) said to the lecturer, "Mr.
> Jones, I have been in a coed school on practice . . . and I found
> that the girls were really more of a nuisance than the boys. You
> have been talking as if the boys could cause trouble but actually
> it's the girls. And I found it more difficult to know what to do
> with them. They were giggling away repeatedly and passing notes
> to the boys, who weren't terribly responsive. It was all a bit awk-
> ward. How would you deal with that?" Jones said, "What I

would do would be to take the two boys nearest to the girls, take
them outside and cane them."

Corporal punishment, then, was intrinsic to the maintenance of order
in secondary schools. The culture of hegemonic masculinity (Connell et al.,
1982) in many (but not all) schools demanded that teachers administer
corporal punishment in order to avoid being positioned as being "weak" or
"soft" by their colleagues and students. Authority was, at least in part,
equated with physical stature and with strength, a quality deemed to be
lacking in women and suspect in men with smaller bodies. Women teachers
who used corporal punishment directly risked being seen as lacking in femininity. Others had to rely on the authority of their male colleagues to
administer it on their behalf. Accustomed to the lore of the cane, some men
found themselves lacking the disciplinary techniques necessary in classrooms of girls where the cane was disallowed. As an act of physical coercion
and as spectacle, corporal punishment can be read as complicit in the construction of embodied masculinity *and* embodied femininity.

While methods of punishment were important in the "hardening" of
men and "domestication" of women, of possibly greater significance were
the sexually differentiated allocations of space — for "discipline proceeds
from the distribution of bodies in space" (Foucault, 1977, p. 141). In his
discussion of French secondary schools in the eighteenth century, Foucault
(1980) wrote that

> one can have the impression that sex was hardly spoken of at all in these
> institutions. But one only has to glance over the architectural layout, the
> rules of discipline, and their whole organization: the question of sex was
> a constant preoccupation. (p. 31)

In the early years of the twentieth century, physical, architectural, and
intellectual spaces were differentially allocated to female and male pupils
and teachers within and by schools. This legacy — as we saw in the previous
chapter — continues today.

The first public and private secondary schools in New Zealand were
single-sex, with a highly academic curriculum. Although the physical excesses of the cultures of only some of the conservative boys schools were
described above, parallel excesses sometimes developed in some of the more
traditional girls schools. Annie Hobson (b. 1912) was a single woman who
had enjoyed teaching during World War II in what was for its time quite a
liberal provincial coeducational school. When the servicemen on the staff
returned, she was required to give up her senior teaching position, and
sought promotion by moving to a metropolitan all-girls school. She was

shocked by the rigidities and the "scattiness" that had been fostered by the static staffing and sex segregation there:

> We'd had a staff room at [the provincial coeducational school]. It was a big comfortable room where we all sat and did our work and had lunch. There was a community of men and women. But at [the metropolitan] Girls' High they had two huge tables jammed into the staff room and you had your own little possie [New Zealand slang for position or place] at one of those. I was sat next to two of the staff who had been there since the year dot. What shocked me was that if a man came into the school it was like a fluttering dovecote. A pair of trousers just set the whole place into a flutter.

In rural districts and towns whose populations were too small to support two single-sex schools, high schools were coeducational. The new metropolitan and provincial technical high schools and junior high schools that were built in the 1920s and 1930s were also coeducational. However, in these it was common practice for girls and boys to be separated for classes as well as for recreation. In the technical high schools, girls and boys took different courses and their class placements, even for general subjects, were based on the fact that girls took commercial or domestic courses, while boys studied for the trades. The English classes taught by Janet Davis (b. 1916) in the early 1950s at an urban technical college were typical: "There were more boys in the senior school than there were girls. I even had separate boys and girls classes. They were doing such separate courses that, even for English, they didn't come together." In 1942–43, Joan Fowler (b. 1930) attended the junior high school section of a provincial coeducational high school and commented that in the first year of the secondary school (third form), only the top academic pupils, those taking Latin, were placed in mixed-sex classes: "You went on to the girls' high school. The intermediate stage had been separated—you were in a girls' class then. So in the third form suddenly acquiring boys in your Latin class I think probably put up the incidence of people wanting to take Latin!" The more academic—potentially middle-class—a student was, the more likely s/he was to experience genuine coeducation.

Not only were the sexes often spatially separated, but facilities, rights, and freedoms accorded them were sometimes unequal (Fry, 1985). Audrey Hall (b. 1928) attended an urban high school from 1942 to 1945, and her comparison of the spatial freedoms permitted girls with those allowed the boys illustrates such inequality:

We had separate entrances, separate areas to the school, separate
playing fields. Girls were second-class citizens. The grounds were
quite extensive, but the girls were confined to an area around the
rose garden, the tennis courts, the basketball courts; although we
went to a park to play basketball. The boys had all the rest, the
lower grounds. The rationale was that the boys sports (football
and so on) took such a lot of room. But this segregation and discrimination continued right through the school. When I became a
prefect I went to see the principal and said that it wasn't fair that
girls had to have written permission to go downtown after school,
but boys could go downtown anyhow. I remember him saying,
"Boys only get into trouble if girls are there, so we have to keep
the girls in the school." I remember that as a very clear example of
discrimination. Instead of saying, "the girls don't get into trouble,
so they can go downtown without permission," they said that the
girls had to have permission, so the boys wouldn't see them downtown!

Similar injustices over inequitable geographical freedoms were described by
Janet Davis (b. 1916) in the case of the technical college in which she was
teaching—a growing high school which was beginning to spread over a
number of campuses:

We were in the buildings in the center of town where the major
part of the staff was. The girls had the only playground; they only
had this very small area. The boys were allowed to go into the
streets and out to a local park. It was felt that the girls needed to
be protected from the big city, and they weren't allowed to go
out.

Students who had boarded in the single-sex dormitories attached to some
secondary schools in towns noted similar differences in the physical freedom permitted to students in the boys and girls dormitories: "The boys at
the hostel [dormitory] had a totally different set of rules to the girls."
Another interviewee mentioned that his father had thought similarly when
he was deciding which secondary schools to send his sons and daughters to:
"My father thought girls had to be protected and boys had to experience
life." Presumably it was women's vulnerability to pregnancy and to rape
that underscored the relative spatial freedoms of men and confinement
(domestication or houseboundness) of women. A double standard was evident.

In this discussion of the period from the 1920s to 1945 I have chosen two themes, both of which have overflowed the temporal constraints of historians: the disciplining of the corporeal bodies of individuals, and the differential and sometimes inequitable allocation of space according to sex. The interviews from which the data quoted here were extracted were structured around the question of how each interviewee's ideas about education had come to form. Some of these stories from teachers (who today are in the 60s to the 90s age range), reveal a "sense of something wrong" (Mitchell, 1973)—a feeling of injustice. During their interviews, some of the men made connections between their experiences with regimes of corporal punishment administered by teachers and prefects and their desire to change things—a desire that became realizable in later years when the availability of less violent disciplinary techniques created the conditions that made possible the abolition of the cane. The women's experiences of confinement in relation to the spatial freedoms offered to men was interpreted by them in their interviews as generative of their desires to make things more equal for women and girls in education. While some of the men quoted here became active in later life in the abolition of the cane, some of the women became active participants in the liberal feminist movement, which was to develop by the late 1960s, for equal opportunities for girls and women in schools.

UNIFORM BODIES?: 1945 TO THE LATE 1960s

Historians and policymakers have often characterized the post–World War II years as heralding progressivist[4] shifts in thinking about, and provisions for, secondary education. The first Labour government was elected in 1935 with a firm socialist agenda of equal opportunities that were to be provided in comprehensive schools. Conceptualizing the binary split between academic and technical education (and children) as inequitable, the government decided to phase out the technical schools and to ensure that technical and academic curricula were taught in the same institutions. The Thomas Committee (Department of Education, 1943) viewed education as a means of producing individuals who would have equal opportunities to succeed within the hierarchies of capitalism and who would also value democracy as a way of life. This equality of opportunity would be accorded to both sexes—both girls and boys would experience all the subjects of the common core curriculum (Middleton, 1988a; 1992c).

However, within this and other key texts of the time, women and girls were also positioned as different from men. As the Thomas Report expressed it, "In addition, every intelligent parent would wish a daughter to have the knowledge, skill and taste to manage a home well and make it a pleasant place to live in" (Department of Education, 1943, p. 17). Domestic science (usually in the form of cooking and sewing classes) was to be made compulsory for all girls. Furthermore, the differential use of masculine, feminine, and gender-neutral pronouns with respect to certain optional subjects conveyed clear assumptions that the physical sciences and mathematical subjects — the most quintessentially rational and disembodied disciplines — would "naturally" be chosen by boys and that the humanities subjects — concerned with the expression of feelings — would naturally be chosen by girls. As Helen May (1992b) has summarized it, the talents and minds of men and women were seen as being "equal but different." The majority of the new secondary schools built to accommodate the children of the postwar baby boom were coeducational, for, as Lyn Yates (1993a) has argued in the case of Australia, the "arguments supporting coeducation as 'natural' were written in a context where relations between men and women were not assumed to be a problem" (p. 97). However, what were assumed to be natural curricular differentiations between the sexes meant that, especially in the technical subjects, a great deal of gender segregation remained.

While the issues discussed in the previous section with respect to the era of the 1920s to 1945 (corporal punishment and the gendered allocation of space) continued to shape students' and teachers' school lives in the postwar decades, I have chosen to emphasize different themes in this section in order to broaden this investigation of the micropractices of disciplinary power. First, I shall raise the question of attitudes towards the biological/reproductive body, and, second, I address the policing of clothing.

In the previous section I overviewed social Darwinist and other scientific/medical notions about the biological body as underpinning the sexual differentiation of secondary school curricula and allocations of space. Although the Victorian and Edwardian eras had generated a plethora of scientific and medical discourses about sex, the subject was not to be mentioned in everyday conversations. In *A History of Sexuality*, Foucault (1980a) argued that "What is peculiar to modern societies . . . is not that they consigned sex to a shadow existence, but that they dedicated themselves to speaking of it *ad infinitum*, while exploiting it as *the* secret" (p. 36; italics in the original). As a doctor of the time put it, "In all groups of women, one finds a surprisingly large number who possess very little, or else a very inaccurate knowledge of their own bodies — or their organs and the function each performs" (Smith, 1942). Many Pakeha children[5] were brought up to think of their genitalia as "private parts"; the acts of urination and defecation as being "rude"; and the issue of where babies come from was often masked in evasions and lies. An illustration of such prudery comes from Mary Donohue (b. 1937), who had attended a provincial girls high school from 1951 to 1955. In keeping with the progressivist ethos which was being disseminated by the Department of Education, Donohue's teacher had taken her biology class out of the school and into the wider community for a field trip:

> We were the first group that ever went out of the school on a trip. We were so excited and so elated about it. We had to make this report to the rest of the school about what we'd done. And so we made up this little review thing. We sang and did all sorts of things in assembly. When we got back in the science lab in the first period after assembly, after this report we'd made for the whole school, Miss March, the headmistress, came in and she just rubbished us. She had the teacher in tears, she had all of us in tears, because in our ditty, we had said that somebody had got locked in the toilets. Miss March said that *no* person ever mentioned the word *toilet* in public. I can still see it — this little lady looking down on these great big girls as if we were the lowest form of crawling creatures. In our little ditties we'd said that somebody had got locked in the toilet on the way up there when we got off the bus, and of course we had this laugh about having to get this person out of the toilet. And because we had mentioned that she had all of us in tears; the whole class in tears, and also the teacher.

In a context in which such reticence on bodily matters was widespread, many young women were ill-prepared for menstruation, and found their first period a terrible shock. The most senior woman in a coeducational school sometimes found her administrative responsibilities centered around the menstruous bodies of girl students. For example, Joan Fowler (b. 1930) described her role as senior mistress in the early years of one of the new coeducational secondary schools that had opened in the postwar years: "The school only had third and fourth formers, so I was teaching third and fourth formers and at the same time getting all the girls in the hall and giving them a little chat on where to buy sanitary towels and things." However, as I will describe in Chapter Three, despite the good intentions of such senior mistresses, the embarrassment associated with menstruation in the 1950s and 1960s continued to make it an uncomfortable experience for many girls.

During those years, evidence of female reproductive sexuality became more visible and acceptable in schools. Before this time, intellectuality/professionality and the expression of female reproductive sexuality had been disursively positioned as contradictory. As has been outlined elsewhere, married women had, during times of economic recession or "oversupply" of teachers, been barred from teaching or from training as teachers (Aitken, 1996; Middleton, 1988b). During the teacher shortages of World War II, married women were "manpowered" back into the classroom, although they were expected to return to the home afterwards. However, the baby boom years of the 1950s and 1960s required the recruitment of married women teachers back into service. Formerly banned from the classroom, women's pregnant and lactating bodies became permissible and visible to students. Margaret Ryan (b. 1938), a mother of five, described how she had combined teaching and the breastfeeding of one of her children up to the age of 6 months:

> They rang and asked me to come back. I said, "Well, look, I've had a baby in the holidays and she isn't even 6 weeks old yet" . . . I didn't fancy taking a 6-week old baby that I was breast-feeding into a classroom, so I employed a housekeeper. . . . You'd feed them at 8 a.m. You'd taken your milk off in the middle of the night before [to leave in a bottle for the housekeeper]. I had to be home by 4. I was oozing milk if I didn't. It worked out quite nicely—it suited me. It wasn't that I chose to go back—I was badgered to go back.

Another source of the beginnings of official acceptance of speaking out about bodily/sexual matters in schools was the introduction of lessons in the biological facts of human reproduction. Recognizing the widespread ignorance of bodily parts and functions, the Thomas Committee had taken the somewhat radical step of advising schools to introduce "lessons in biology and in the anatomy and physiology of the reproductive system" (Department of Education, 1943, p. 53). Teenagers' knowing the scientific facts was supposed to ensure that they made the rational choice to abstain from sexual intercourse (Fine, 1988; Trudell, 1992). The onus for such rational choice was placed on girls, whose "desire for sexual intercourse" was seen as being less than that of boys, in whom, according to the Department of Health (1955), "sexual desire is aroused much more easily" (p. 7). This reversed the usual binary in which mind was constituted as masculine and the body as feminine. Within this rationalist/scientific discourse of sex education, the good woman (or the virgin) was positioned as the agent of (rational) self-control and the man as a potential victim of bodily desires, which could be controlled with the help of this good woman. The girl who acted on her own desires, or who "gave in" to the desires of the male was seen as lacking. Either she was deficient by nature—she had an unnatural and therefore unfeminine sex drive—or she was lacking in moral character, in self-control.

Although I do not have data on this in the present study, in one of my previous studies (Middleton, 1985; 1987/94) Maori and Pakeha women described how the sexual double standard was stratified by the practice of school streaming (tracking by subject choice, measured ability, or both). There are suggestions that, in at least some schools, girls in the lower (domestic science or typing) streams were stereotyped by top stream (Latin and French) girls as more sexually promiscuous than their academic peers (Middleton, 1985; 1987/1994). Although there is no statistical evidence that this was so, the school resistance strategies of some lower stream girls may have fuelled this perception: telling more "rude jokes," swearing more, and violating dress codes in a "sexier" manner than did their more "lady-like" counterparts in top streams.

Maori girls, clustered in lower streams, were sometimes positioned, as one informant put it, along "the class, race, sexuality dimension. We were brown sluts, *bags*." The positioning of indigenous, Black, and "oriental" men and women as more highly sexually charged than white men and women—this as a legacy of colonialism—has been an object of research by Black and postcolonial scholars of both sexes (Bhabha, 1994; Davis, 1981). Such attitudes are traces of the earlier discursive regime which conceptualized hereditary "degeneracy" as being at the root of class and racial inequalities (Eldred-Grigg, 1984; D. Jones, 1990; Parkinson, 1991).

In 1954 the sexual double standard was given a powerful boost in the report of the Mazengarb Committee, which had been set up by the government after several "moral panics" (Shuker, 1987) over the overt, and sometimes so-called deviant, sexual activities of teenagers. One of these was the scandal over the Parker-Hume case, which was recently immortalized in Peter Jackson's award-winning movie, *Heavenly Creatures*. Two girls from the city of Christchurch had murdered the mother of one of them; their "unnatural" and "deviant" lesbianism was blamed for this atrocity (Glamuzina & Laurie, 1991). In the same year there was another scandal when a group of girls and boys in the Hutt Valley (a Wellington suburb) were truant from school and, in the quaint terminology of the 1950s, "acquired unlawful carnal knowledge" of one another. The scandal echoed round the globe:

It was the Mazengarb Report . . . the "immorality" in Lower Hutt. I was on a train in England, in a sleeper. A woman was reading a paper on the other bunk. And she said, "Are you a New Zealander?" and I said, "Yes." She said, "Well, there's something going on in New Zealand, in Lower Hutt. Where's Lower Hutt?" I said it was by Wellington. It was headlines in the English papers!

The necessity for adults to police the sexual knowledge and activities of adolescents was taken so seriously that the government distributed the Mazengarb Committee's (1954) *Report on Moral Delinquency in Children and Adolescents* to every New Zealand family. "Nowadays," warned the committee, "girls do not always wait for an advance to be made to them, nor are they reticent as they used to be in discussing sexual matters with the opposite sex. It is unfortunate that in many cases girls, by immodest conduct, have become the leaders in sexual misbehaviour and have in many cases corrupted the boys" (p. 15). It is hardly surprising that these ideas resulted in a renewed enthusiasm for the spatial segregation of the sexes by means of single-sex schools. Waiwhetu Girls' High School was opened in the Hutt Valley, and in several cities and provincial towns whose secondary-school-age population was outgrowing their sole secondary school's buildings, the decision was to divide the coeducational school into two single-sex schools rather than to add a new coeducational school.

It is in the context of this discussion about how the embodied sexualities of teenage girls and boys were regarded that I shall raise the question of the normalizing of dress in schools. As in Britain and Australia (Meadmore and Symes, 1996), New Zealand secondary schools have a long tradition of uniform requirements and the strict policing of these—a process which continued unchanged during the postwar years. To illustrate the rigidities of the regulation of students' dress, let me flash back in time to World War II. Audrey Hall (b. 1928) recalled that no relaxation in uniform regulations had been permitted to accommodate the bodily discomforts caused by the impact of the rationing of coal:

> There was no heating. It was frosty in the morning and every morning we used to run around the block to get us warm for the rest of the day. . . . We all wore mittens, black woollen mittens. You had to have the right color, you couldn't have colored mittens, and you couldn't have colored hair ribbons or anything like that.

Girls' school uniforms included gloves and berets in winter and Panama hats in summer. Boys had to wear caps. Janet Fowler (b. 1916) recalled being interviewed in 1959 for a principal's job in a provincial girls school: "I can remember being asked such stupid questions, like did I think the girls should wear hats and gloves? I think I agreed that they should wear hats, although I disposed of hats after I got there. But I think I was a bit *toey* about gloves."

There were dress codes for teachers too. Some rebelled against what they saw as the overregulation of their dress. Ngaire Donaldson (b. 1938) taught home economics, which had a strict dress code for its staff as well as its students:

> I found the subject to be quite uninspiring to teach. I broke all the rules. I had students rushing around not in white aprons—I had them rushing around in all sorts of different-colored aprons. That upset the inspectors. Not only was the teacher not in white, but she had her students not in them. I upset them further because my sewing machines had creative soft sculpture as their machine covers.

Uniform requirements went beyond clothing; schools had rules about hairstyles as well. A dramatic vignette comes from an interview with Sean O'Leary (b. 1951), whose first two years of secondary schooling, from 1964 to 1965, were in the hands of Catholic priests:

> There was a thing about hair being cut straight—*straight backs*—you weren't allowed them. A few of us, who were getting into that rebellious age, got them. During the day we were all picked out one by one and taken up to the discipline master, who was waiting in the place where the priests used to live. I remember going up the tower, knock, knock, and into a dark room. And there he was with a chair in the middle, ready with all his haircutting material and he cut my hair. I didn't have long hair, it was just a straight back. As you can imagine, he did a rough job and I just felt terrible after it.

To summarize: the post–World War II years saw some relaxation in the official silences concerning bodily matters. Although the sexual double standard remained firmly in place, there were the beginnings of a speaking out and an increasing acceptance of the visibility of (married) women's reproductive sexuality—pregnancy and lactation. The splitting off of mind from body in the official rationalist discourses of education, and the attempts to force bodies into a normalized image which denied the individual's rights to the kinds of freedom of expression which liberal/progressive discourse encouraged were beginning to be undermined. This contradiction was described by some as formative of critiques that were to be collectively expressed in the neoprogressivist educational discourses and the multiple protest movements of the late 1960s and early 1970s.

PROTESTS: FROM THE MID-1960s TO THE LATE 1980s

During the 1960s many of the post–World War II baby boom generation—students whose parents may not have had access to higher, or even
secondary, education—were moving to the cities and studying in tertiary
institutions. The sense of marginality many of us who were such students
felt in academic environments—as female, Maori, working-class, and so
on—together with the knowledge of possibilities afforded us by the economic prosperity of the time fuelled radical critiques of education and wider
social protests. The hippy movement, the student revolts, anti–Vietnam
War protests, ideas from the U.S. civil rights movement, Maori national-
ism, antiapartheid demonstrations, and the beginnings of second-wave feminism all had their repercussions on school students and teachers.

Demographic changes gave impetus to the articulation of the various
protests and critiques. In the late 1960s, secondary schools were faced with
increasingly diverse populations of students as a result of the urbanization
of Maori and the immigration of Pacific Islanders. Teachers—as individuals, within their schools and professional organisations—struggled to come
to terms with how best to teach in schools with such diverse student populations. The retired principal of a metropolitan girls high school described the
visual changes to the school as viewed from the stage at morning assembly:

> By 1970 it was a different school. You could stand on the stage
> and you could look at the school. The hair color was different.
> Whereas it had been sort of light brown, the occasional blonde,
> and the occasional redhead, it was a much darker mix with the
> Chinese and the Indian and the Greek and the Pacific Islanders
> coming in. And at the same time as we were realizing that our
> school was changing we were looking at major changes in educa-
> tional direction, and I'm really always heartened that it was teach-
> ers that took the plunge. Because *Education in Change* was a key-
> note document, I think.

Education in Change was published in 1969 by the New Zealand Post-
Primary Teachers' Association (NZPPTA) (the secondary school teachers
union). Its recommendations were in tune with the "neoprogressivist"[6]
thinking which was being disseminated and taken up by the more liberal
secondary teachers—particularly in English and social studies (Middleton,
1996d). These ideas were compatible with those appearing in several influential new American and British books for teachers—part of a new wave of
affordable paperbacks, produced by multinational publishing companies,
that poured into the country during the early 1970s. Written by teachers

for teachers, they discussed, among other issues, how to tailor programs to the individual interests of students (e.g., Holt, 1974; Kohl, 1969; Postman & Weingartner, 1971).

Education in Change encapsulated some of this thinking in the following definition: "Education forms a major part in the process of individual and social growth and should be self-motivating because its rewards are inherent. This report is directed towards the development of a concept of self-motivated learning" (New Zealand Post-Primary Teachers' Association, 1969, p. xiv). It lists "human qualities which education should be concerned to promote at all times. The highest value is placed on: the urge to enquire; concern for others; the desire for self-respect" (p. 1). By the early 1970s, the Department of Education was introducing new syllabi in which the postwar discourse of equality as sameness gave way to one of education for diversity—cultural pluralism and student choice within the system and some support for the creation of educational alternatives.

In the more liberal/progressive schools, these ideas generated major upheavals in the ways they were structured, and this brought about changes in teaching practice. Up until this time what had counted as academic had rested on the cognitive styles, habitus, and interests of the white professional and managerial elite (Bourdieu, 1971). Since the development of psychology as a discipline in the 1930s, students had been allocated to courses and streams largely on the basis of their scores on intelligence tests. As a means of ensuring justice and equality of opportunity, these had been believed to be scientific and therefore as appropriately objective measures of innate potential (Olssen, 1988). The social Darwinism of the 1920s and 1930s had left unquestioned the resulting relegation of Maori and working-class Pakeha to the manual streams—a stratification that became increasingly obvious as the processes of urbanization brought about the influx of brown students into the predominantly white secondary schools and universities (A. Jones, 1991).

Conceptualizing cultural difference as valuable diversity rather than as deviance or inferiority, the discourse of pluralism provoked some schools to destream during the 1970s. This breakdown in the barriers between students who took different courses (academic, home economics, commercial, agricultural, or industrial) resulted in coeducational classes of mixed ability and mixed race. It thus altered previous patterns of the differential distributions of groups of students in school space. Teaching in non-streamed classes made whole-class instruction difficult and forced secondary teachers to develop the kinds of individualized and small-group teaching methods which up until this time had been characteristic only of primary schools (Middleton & May, 1997).

From the point of view of the discipline of the body it would seem that progressivism—which rests on assumptions of freedom of choice, intrinsic motivation, and self-discipline—is in direct opposition to some traditional school regulatory practices of, for example, students' dress, that we have seen so far in these two chapters. However, as Valerie Walkerdine has argued (1984, 1987, 1992; Walkerdine & Lucey, 1989), what happens is that the processes of discipline, regulation, and normalization become more covert: "The child supposedly freed by this process to develop according to its nature was the most classified, catalogued, watched and monitored in history. Freed from coercion, the child was much more subtly regulated into normality" (Walkerdine, 1992, p. 18). Within a progressivist school environment, Walkerdine argues, "discipline became not overt disciplining, but covert watching . . . [as] the classroom became the facilitating space for each individual under the watchful and total gaze of the teacher" (p. 19). Writing about child-centered learning in primary schools, Walkerdine noted that the freedom of children meant less space for the teacher, who became "the servant of the omnipotent child, whose needs she must meet at all times" (p. 21).

In accordance with this shift, new social technologies for regulating the population without physical coercion were becoming more freely available to teachers (Walkerdine, 1984). Behaviorist psychology with its techniques of positive reinforcement was being taught in teachers colleges and universities. The new psychological and sociological discourses positioned "problem" students not as naughty but as having behavioral difficulties that were often the result of social pathology. Accordingly, many schools created senior staffing positions that were devoted to the welfare of students and their families. Eric Cotton (b. 1939) described the burn out he experienced as a dean in 1971 at a new coeducational school with a high population of working-class immigrant Pacific Island students and a senior mistress who had failed to win the confidence of Samoan girls:

> I was a dean and that was a huge job there, if you wanted to make it that way. I would spend day after day looking for girls around the town. They could be in any situation and anywhere, and I saw the rougher side of life that I didn't even think existed. I got on really well with girls—basically because the woman who was a senior mistress found it difficult and was confrontational with them all the time. I would be in my classroom, and there'd be a knock on the door and there'd be one of the girls there saying, "We need to see you for a moment." And no one knew about it. So I'd leave some work for the class and say, "What's your problem?" Mainly Samoan girls, who were getting a really hard time at home. They'd say, "We've got this problem." "Where-

abouts are you? How many of you?" They'd usually have gone
into the girls toilet.

This welfare, or social work, model—characteristic of today's secondary
schools, as argued in the previous chapter—became dominant in the official
discourses about discipline in schools during this period.

In the remainder of this discussion on the period from the late 1960s to
the late 1980s, I shall develop further the two themes introduced in the
previous section on the postwar years: the regulation of clothing and discourses concerning the handling of sexual/bodily matters in the curriculum.

The more neoprogressive schools (some remained largely untouched
by neoprogressivism) were characterized by increasing informality in relationships between students and teachers. Individualized and group teaching
methods encouraged more fluidity of seating arrangements and movement
in the classroom by students and teachers. Seeking bodily comfort, freedom
of movement, and informality, some of us who were teaching at this time
struggled to loosen the rigidities of our schools' requirements with respect
to the way we dressed. I had male colleagues who refused to wear ties, grew
their hair and sideburns, and wore jeans. We younger women found that
our miniskirts conflicted with the freedom of movement required in the
classroom—as Rona Gregg (b. 1948) explained: "In those days you had
miniskirts and when you lifted your hand up to write on the blackboard, it
wasn't a particularly good thing to be doing!" The revealing tendencies of
the miniskirts of the early 1970s no doubt, at least in part, influenced the
acceptance at this time of trousers as appropriate work clothes for female
teachers.

The influx of young and fashionable baby boomers into secondary
school teaching in the 1970s exacerbated classroom management dilemmas
for one of my interviewees, whose embodied sexuality did not match her
students' ideals. Audrey Hall (b. 1928) had always taught in girls schools
before taking on a position at the age of 49 in a coeducational school in a
conservative suburb:

> I found boys very lazy as students. A lot of them never settled
> down and did a decent period of work, or their homework. I was
> older by then. A younger teacher can get a rapport with students,
> almost a hero worship. They see you as a role model and notice
> what you're wearing, and comment on it, too—quite a different
> sort of relationship. But coming in as a middle-aged woman to
> boys classes you really had to be very bossy and authoritarian . A
> feeling of "we're all in this together, let's get to work" didn't seem

to work. I like a relaxed way of teaching, but I found that at that school I had to be very authoritarian.

The publication in New Zealand of an English translation of the Danish-authored *Little Red Schoolbook* (Hansen & Jensen, 1972) brought the language of liberation from the social protest movements into the context of schools. In a climate in which students' rights were seen as important, some students challenged inconsistencies between the stance of freedom of expression that was offered to them by the liberal/progressive and protest movement discourses and their positioning as passive recipients of teachers' normalizing practices. While some liberal schools relaxed uniform and hair regulations, conservative ones maintained them, even in the face of student protest. Robert Williams (b. 1939) describes one example in a coeducational school: "*The Little Red Schoolbook* came out—ideas about pupil power and this sort of stuff. But it died a natural death fairly quickly. I can remember when the Beatles came out, we had all the fuss about long hair." However, at his next school (a boys school), the struggle had become more confrontational:

> The former principal had had the school absolutely screwed
> down tight, and the new principal was faced with mutiny from
> the boys—sit-ins on the school field over caps. He abolished caps,
> and the board of governors thought that that was the end of the
> world. The sit-ins were about wearing caps, and long hair and all
> that stuff. It was the time of the *Little Red Schoolbook,* a time of
> great ferment. Student power.

The refusal of some schools to relax their uniform requirements trivialized them as educational institutions for some of their more questioning students. For example, Nell Wilson (b. 1955) attended an urban coeducational school from 1968 to 1971 and resisted the minutiae of the school's attempt to normalize every inch of her bodily adornment:

> The uniform was a gray skirt and a white blouse. So I made a tie-
> dye gray skirt which didn't go down well at all. I was constantly
> called into the senior mistress's office and given lectures. . . . I
> chose to ignore all of that. All of these things had nothing to do
> with what went on in the classroom, but they were all of the
> things that were actually important as an adolescent, I think. And
> as a fourth former I had quite long hair, and so I used to wear it
> in all different kinds of ways. And I remember distinctly—this is
> one of those things that you never forget—we had a "gals" assem-

bly and Mrs Owens (who was the dragon) walked up and down the aisles and picked out girls who had to go on stage for having inappropriate hairstyles. That included me, who on this particular day had these pigtails just above my ears—my hair was really long, so it kind of looked like Pippi Longstocking pan handles. . . . I think as a result of things like that, I was so sick of the place that I didn't do a seventh form [senior] year.

Some schools at this time abolished uniform. While for many, this may have signaled an increase in personal freedom, for others—especially those whose families were unable to provide them with good clothing—it was a source of constraint and discomfort. Rangi Davidson (b. 1956), who had himself attended a private Maori boys boarding school, had regarded his own school's uniform as important in helping him to develop a sense of self-worth:

> I'm basically a traditionalist and a disciplinarian. . . . I like to wear a tie for school. I believe in the importance of a uniform for self-esteem and all that sort of thing. The uniform gives you a sense of belonging to something and if it's a nice uniform it makes you feel good. The same as dressing. If you dress well, you feel good. If you don't dress well, you don't feel so good.

In the late 1980s, Rangi had taken a senior position in a Maori bilingual unit. Bilingual classes and units (departments) in mixed schools, and separate Maori-language immersion preschools and schools, were established in the 1980s as a result of the protests and initiatives of Maori people. They claimed separate spaces for Maori linguistic and cultural maintenance, and to foster their self-determination and political autonomy (Irwin, 1990; Smith, 1990; L. Smith, 1993). The unit in which Rangi taught was in a large coeducational school which had abolished uniforms. The school had a high proportion of students from homes in which parents and caregivers were on low incomes or unemployed, and the students he taught were mainly from such backgrounds. Concerned about the self-image of the students in the bilingual unit, Rangi introduced a special traveling uniform for them:

> I enjoyed working in a big school. Over 1,000 kids. Coed, my first coed school. Nonuniform. A few things there that were really new to me. . . . After a while it didn't worry me, the uniform— essentially I am a traditionalist. I really believe in that. But what I tried to do to get around it was, I introduced uniforms. The bilingual kids had a travelling uniform. Essentially I was just worried

about the bilingual kids, I wasn't worried about the rest of the
school. And when the kids traveled they looked nice and they felt
good about themselves.

The freedom of students from affluent families to choose their own dress
was at the expense of those less well-off—it accentuated the signs of their
poverty.

Not only did student-centeredness influence the regulation of bodily
adornment, but it also gave form to new discourses about the ways the
physical body itself could be spoken about in schools. During the 1970s, the
spirit of neoprogressivism—centered as it was on humanist psychological
concepts of personal growth—had extended into the question of sexuality
education. No longer conceptualized in terms of introducing students to the
biological facts alone, sexuality education was viewed as being part of a
broader education in human development and relationships, values, and
health (Brett, 1996; Trudell, 1992). These ideas were developed in the
context of the "second wave" of feminism (Department of Education,
1976a) and several reports of the time implied, even if they did not always
say so directly, that capacities for sexual arousal and expression were
equally distributed between women and men (Department of Education,
1977). Emotions and desires were no longer missing (Fine, 1988) from the
discourse.

During the time of the postpill "sexual revolution," speaking openly
about sex in the mass media became increasingly tolerated (see Chapter
Three). Commercial publishers marketed sexual information for teenagers,
this often including the formerly taboo subjects of sexual desire, masturbation, contraception, homosexuality, and abortion. This created new, easily
accessible, conduits for teenagers themselves to access information without
mediation or moralizing by adults (e.g., Hansen & Jensen, 1972; Tuohy &
Murphy, 1976). The question of sexuality education became the object of
intense media speculations, meetings by concerned parents, and staffroom
discussions. Several major government reports on secondary education
were produced within this context, and the language used in these shows
the influence of these wider community debates and concerns (Department
of Education, 1976b, 1977).

The Johnson Report expressed some of the more open sexual attitudes
of the time as follows:

No students should leave school without facing up to the real implications
of personal relationships, and the consequences to their own personality
development if they fail to do this. We want students to realise that

sexuality involves self-discipline and involves loving and caring for another person—not the mere seeking of self-release. It is the basis of a
lasting relationship; it is a most powerful emotional drive and has a
great capacity for bringing happiness and giving meaning to life. It is not
confined to the younger years but grows with understanding and maturity. It can be a spiritual force. (Department of Education, 1977, p. 38)

On the basis of their knowledge that teenagers always have been, and
always will be, sexually active, the Johnson Committee's focus was on
urging them to confine such activities to "caring relationships." However,
because they did not say that teenagers should be taught that sex belongs
only in marriage, the message was too permissive for many and caused a
public outcry. Upon the appointment of a conservative minister of education by the National government in the early 1980s, the "moral Right"
pressure groups (influenced by the U.S. moral majority movement) were
able to play a major part in ensuring that the Johnson Report was never
implemented (Openshaw, 1983; Ryan, 1988). Its language, however, encapsulated the ethos which underpinned the many (and often coeducational) "human relationships" programs which were introduced into secondary schools during the 1970s and 1980s (Department of Education, 1977)
and which have continued to be in place in at least some secondary schools
up to the present day (Brett, 1996; Education Review Office, 1996).

DISCUSSION

This brings me full circle in this history of the present—back to the
mid-1980s, where Chapter One began. My aim has been to describe empirically, in Foucauldian terms, the intersecting of "power-knowledges" and
the everyday surveillance and disciplining of the (male and female) bodies
of students and teachers in secondary schools. Accordingly, I have focused
on the relations of surveillance that are, of necessity, at the heart of the
practice of teaching: "the supervision of the smallest fragment of life, or of
the body" (Foucault, 1977, p. 140). As policymakers and historians have
demonstrated, there have been changes in the grand theories, or regimes of
truth, that have driven the design of schooling: Notions that advanced
levels of schooling were for the fittest (the elite) were superseded by more
egalitarian ideals. Coercion through physical violence (use of the cane) gave
way to techniques of behavior modification. Berets and caps were replaced
by more informal dress. But what have remained constant, as Foucault has
argued, are the broad mechanisms of administrative/disciplinary power.
Stephen Ball (1990) explains:

In the processes of schooling the student is compiled and constructed both
in the passive processes of identification, and in an active, self-forming
subjectification, the latter involving processes of self-understanding mediated by an external authority figure—for our purposes, most commonly
the teacher. For example, this is apparent in the increasing use of profiling
and records. (p. 4)

Yet teachers and students are not mere passive victims of monitoring
and regulation. My data include many examples of protest and rebellion,
critique and creativity, on the part of both students and teachers. Within
the disciplinary apparatuses, people have access to multiple discourses and,
as creative strategists, construct unique amalgams of theories and practices.
As well as the dominant discourses, or regimes of truth, there are "subjugated knowledges" (Foucault, 1977; 1980b). To offer a case study, in the
following chapter I shall explore the emerging feminist discourses as they
were created and lived during the years of the sexual revolution.

I began this chapter with the conceptual map drawn by some of New
Zealand's historians and policymakers. A map positions the mapmaker
outside or above the terrain being drawn (Rose, 1993; Sibley, 1995); the
tides and currents of educational thought are surveyed from the top. Similarly, sociologists, critical theorists, and feminists often work in terms of
grand narratives—ideology, patriarchy, hegemony, and so forth—and force
their data into these categories. Foucault (1980b) advised against this way
of going about social research. We should not, he said, focus too much on
constructing grand narratives about "the regulated and legitimate forms of
power in their central locations" (p. 96) but, rather, study empirically the
everyday workings out of the operation and channelling of power on the
ground—"with power at its extremities, in its ultimate destinations, with
those points where it becomes capillary, that is, in its more regional and
local forms of institutions" (p. 96)

As my data have shown, the maps of the historians (as do the schemas
of sociologists) impose an artificial order on the untidiness of everyday life.
The discourses of policy texts should be studied, but in relation to life on
the ground. Policies that work in the sense of people working according to
them are not mere impositions from above, for, as Foucault (1980b) argued, "in order for there to be a movement from above to below there has
to be a capillarity from below to above at the same time" (p. 142).

CHAPTER THREE

Swinging Chicks?:
Sex Education, Feminists, and
the Sexual Revolution

In Chapters One and Two, I mapped the broad tides and currents of disciplining sexuality in secondary schools in the twentieth century. While my readings of policy documents provided a view of these from the top, excerpts from longer life-histories offered a view from the bottom. An electronic database of transcripts from 75 teachers enabled me to focus cross-sectionally on slices of time through the eyes of men and women of different age groups. In interviews that were not framed around questions of sex itself, but about experiences of schooling and the formation of the teachers' educational philosophies, it is interesting that so many of their stories were about bodily matters. To learn about the more intimate dimensions of students' and teachers' lives—those we refer to as our sexual experiences—I must now use different data.

In 1982 and 1983 I interviewed 12 feminist teachers, each of them several times. My questions were centered on how and why they had come to develop their (liberal and/or Marxist and/or Maori and/or radical, separatist, anarchist, etc.) feminist educational theories and how these influenced their educational practice (Middleton, 1985). In the course of the interviews, these women talked a great deal about their sexual/bodily experiences. Their experiences of sexual contradictions, sexual discrimination/oppression, and sexual marginalities, they said, had been generative of their feminist positions.

This data offers the opportunity for a shift in my focus on both time and space. The view is through only 12 women's eyes—13 if I include my own, since I was very much part of the events I am studying here. I do not have comparable data for men—men's sexual experiences during this time must await another study. While the teachers in previous chapters were of many different ages, the 12 women discussed here were all around the same age—born immediately after World War II. I view—instead of a wide-angled cross section of, say, a decade—a 30-year timespan as a developmental progression from the women's childhoods in the 1950s until the time they were in their early thirties in the early 1980s. My framing of space is wider, for rather than confining my sights to the school as an encapsulated site of regulatory practices, I look across multiple sites.

What was it like to grow up at this time? How was the disciplining of the sexual body lived out by the generation who were born just after World War II—children in the 1950s, teenagers in the 1960s, and young adults in the 1970s? In particular, I am interested in what is often referred to as the sexual revolution—a time of liberalization of attitudes toward sex education and speaking about bodily parts and of a greater tolerance towards sexual activities and orientations other than those occurring in monogamous marriage—the point where Chapter Two concluded. Were the sixties really "swinging," as they are sometimes characterized by today's young people?

As in previous chapters, I shall weave through my counterpoint a strong thread of Foucault. How useful is his work in understanding women's lives? And what does it offer in the theorization of case studies? Is it of value to those who wish to study feminism as a social phenomenon or who frame their research through feminist eyes? Many feminist writers have drawn on Foucault's work, usually in combination with psychoanalysis (Flax, 1990; Grosz, 1989), classical or neo-Marxism (Barrett, 1991; Hennessey, 1993), or French poststructuralist literary theory (Nicholson, 1990; Weedon, 1987). Within the field known variously as the "sociology of women's education" or "education feminism" (Stone, 1994), many feminists have drawn on some or all of these combinations. While the writers with a more literary/psychoanalytic emphasis are commonly termed *feminist poststructuralists* (Davies, 1989); the term *feminist materialist* is being increasingly used to refer to those who blend Foucauldian analysis with Marxist or neo-Marxist concepts (Kenway, 1990; Lather, 1990; Middleton, 1993b, 1995; A. Jones, 1991, 1993; Weiler, 1988; Weiner, 1994; Yates, 1993b; Walkerdine, 1987, 1992). The enthusiasm for various Foucauldian-feminist blends is by no means universal. Camille Paglia (1995) condemns Foucault as "one of the most misogynist writers of the past one hundred years; there isn't a single woman anywhere in his books" (p. 461). She comments that "*Dante's Inferno* has a special reserved foxhole for the followers of Lacan, Derrida, and Foucault, who will burn for eternity in their own verbal sludge" (p. 408).

Bearing this challenge in mind, I shall weave through my analysis the four great strategies of power which Foucault (1980a) identified as characterizing the construction of the embodied phenomenon known as sexuality in the modern age (since the eighteenth century) in Western societies: a pedagogization of children's sex, a hysterization of women's bodies, a socialization of procreative behaviour, and a psychiatrization of perverse pleasure (p. 104). I begin with an overview of the 12 women's experiences of the social construction of their female sexualities during childhood and adolescence. I then create case studies which outline the various sexual contradictions as experienced by five individual women and describe the strategies that they, as individuals, developed in their sexual and professional lives to resolve them.

A PAINFUL PERIOD: DISCIPLINING PUBERTY

For some, puberty marked a time of increasing restriction on personal and physical freedom. In the 1950s and early 1960s, what Foucault (1980a) described as Victorian attitudes towards the body still prevailed. In 1937, Clara Thomson, an American psychoanalyst, described these attitudes:

> The changes brought about by cultural restrictions at the girls' puberty are not of a superficial nature. At this time in the Victorian picture a girl passed from a position of relative equality with boys to one of inferiority. . . . especially in her sexual life her freedom of development was curbed. The punishment for spontaneous expression of sexual interests was very great. One impulsive act resulting in pregnancy could ruin a girl's whole life. Her training was in the direction of insincerity about her sexual interests. She was taught to be ashamed of menstruation. It was something to be concealed and any accident leading to its discovery was especially humiliating. In short, womanhood began with much unpleasantness. It was characterised by feelings of body shame, loss of freedom, loss of equality with boys, and loss of the right to be aggressive. (Thomson, 1937/1971, p. 132)

My interviewees' stories supported this claim. Several former tomboys spoke of their parents' attempts to "feminize" them into "young ladies." Many spoke of new restrictions on the amount of contact they had with boys. No longer their playmates, their equals, boys were to be feared as possible "impregnators." The transition to secondary school occurred around the time of puberty. For tomboys, being sent to an all-girls school could be traumatic. Conversely, others described being sent to coeducational schools and their difficulties in maintaining a pattern of acceptance as one of the boys in subcultures in which some boys positioned girls as submissive and "scatty" sexual objects.

Menstruation is a biological experience shared by all women at an important stage of their lives. Although many cultures regard the menses as an important *rite de passage* (de Beauvoir, 1949/1971), in the New

Zealand Pakeha culture of the late 1950s, menstruation was often a source of shame and embarrassment, many girls resenting it and the inescapable proof of femaleness it offers. This may not necessarily apply to Maori women.[1] Autobiographies (Frame, 1983) and sociological research give evidence of negative feelings towards menstruation on the part of Pakeha women of the postwar (and earlier) generations. Despite the postwar encouragement of schools and parents to teach children the (biological/scientific) facts of life, this "medicalization of sex" (Foucault, 1980a) rendered invisible feelings and emotions. In Michelle Fine's (1988) terms, the "discourse of desire" was "missing." In the early 1980s, a survey of 100 women noted:

> It is true that most of the younger women were better prepared for puberty than women 30 years ago, but it was disturbing to find that biological details about the changes in women's bodies were still inadequately explained. Even those who knew what to expect physically had little indication from their parents that there might be changes in how they felt. (Barrington & Gray, 1981, p. 36)

A description of the unpleasantness of menstruation was offered by Kathleen, who had not been told the biological facts before she started menstruating:

> When you had your period you lived in fear of it ever going through your school smock, your pinafore, and someone finding out. Because, you see, you didn't realize that other people got it as well. . . . My mother's exact wording was, "If you bleed, come and tell me." Now that could have been my finger or my big toe— I didn't know. I did vaguely know something—I can remember sanitary pads, but I never associated that with young women. I associated it with older women. So, when I actually did get my period and woke up one morning and was in dreadful agony I actually went to my father, and I thought I was dying. And I said to him, "I'm bleeding." And of course he, in shock and horror, immediately told my mother to get out of bed and fix me up. So, you see, you were kept in ignorance . . . you didn't talk about it, and didn't talk about it among your friends.

The experience was made more unpleasant by the inadequate materials available. Many of the women's mothers, being of a generation of women who were kept in ignorance about their bodies, considered tampons to be for married women only. So schoolgirls usually had to use bulky sanitary pads, belts, and pins. Leslie, who attended a large city girls school described the discomforts of an inadequate technology and the embarrassment of cultural taboos in the school setting:

> We had a bit of a brief explanation about how to get sanitary towels from toilets. They had a vending machine in the toilets, you needed seven pence [pennies were large copper coins]. You can imagine how many kids would be carrying seven pennies with them, which meant you had to get some money, you then had to take it to the office, to get it changed into your seven pennies by the school secretary. She was lovely, but just that action of having to get together this money, take it there, go to put seven clunky pennies into this bloody machine; I never once used it and I don't think many of my friends did either. We had these horrible gym slips in the summer which were a light blue and we'd have to sit for hours during the day. Of course menstrual blood would just soak right through. It would soak into my uniform. I'd be stuck at school with no way of getting any other towels or anything like that being too shy and too ill at ease to go and get new towels. So that sometimes I would go through the day incredibly uncomfortable and with my uniform just covered in blood behind. It was really horrible. I hated that.

Only 2 of the 12 women had attended schools where menstruation was discussed openly by teachers. Interestingly, these were both new coeducational schools. One woman described how her physical education teacher had told the girls, in a class where boys were present, about the benefits of physical exercise during menstruation. Another had a full sex education program in a mixed-sex situation at school. It may have been that the newer schools, with younger staff, were more likely to implement the recommendations and spirit of the Thomas Report on sex education. The other women either had no sex education at school, apart from the mandatory general science lessons on reproduction, or a single talk by a doctor or district nurse, an experience that was seen as embarrassing to all concerned and where issues of sexual behavior and morality were avoided—sex was a medical issue (Foucault, 1980a).

Few told stories of positive feelings about beginning menstruation and about female sexuality in general. Linda saw her parents as unusually liberal for the time. Her father, a social worker, had been closely involved in his daughters' sex education and the occasion of the onset of menstruation was given the dignity of a rite of passage:

My parents were very determined that us kids had healthy attitudes to our bodies and sexuality. My mother always taught how her mother had been committed to that too because she'd had such awful experiences with knowing nothing and starting to bleed and thinking she was dying from a bleeding wound and things like that. Both of them wanted to be sure that we felt good about ourselves. The dinner table was always a place where we talked about everything and so, when I was eleven and started to menstruate I certainly knew everything about it and saw it as a time to celebrate. My parents wanted to have a celebration of some sort, so I was able to choose to go and see Helen Shapiro [a British pop star]. But I got the mumps and didn't go, so my next choice was to go and see Howard Morrison, the Howard Morrison Quartet [a Maori pop group]. Went along and had a wonderful time.

However, Linda was aware that her family's attitudes were unusual:

To me it was a lovely thing to start menstruating and I felt really good about it and very aware that for my friends it was very different thing. It was sort of hidden and not known about. So I was aware that what was happening to me and my family was slightly different to what was happening in other families.

In general, then, the experience of menstruation was very much a negative one. Far from glorying in their womanhood, these feminist women described their memories about puberty as a time of restriction, shame, and being cut off from open relationships with men, since menstruation was usually seen as being a private matter for women only. However, one of the Maori women told of how when she had first menstruated, her father had explained it to her, suggesting that the negative connotations of menstruation may be a Pakeha phenomenon (Pere, 1988). This description of the discursive construction of menstruation is important in its analysis of normal embodied womanhood as something dirty or shameful. For girls who rejected the dominant ideology of domestic femininity, or sex roles, this might well have further reinforced negative images of what it meant to be an adult woman.

VIRGINS AND BIRTHS

During their school years, all 12 of the women in this study had perceived overt heterosexuality as having some negative consequences. Three commonly mentioned examples were their perceptions of their mothers' lives as unhappy or unfulfilled and their determination not to follow their examples, the association of overt heterosexual activity with girls in the lower streams, and the stigma attached to those young girls who became unmarried mothers. These perceptions strongly reinforced any religious or other moral beliefs the women were taught regarding the importance of premarital virginity.

Examples of the women's perceptions of their mothers' lives included: mothers whose appearance and demeanor, or habitus, in Bourdieu's (1971) terms, was seen as inappropriate for a dairy farming community: too educated, too artistic, too fashionable. Those with mothers who had higher educational qualifications than had their fathers expressed concern that their mothers had abandoned any career ambitions upon marriage. Their mothers' careers had been subordinate to those of their fathers, even though, in one case, the mother was the better teacher. All 12 women perceived their mothers' lives as in some sense unhappy, frustrated, or unfulfilled. Reasons given for this were the lack of educational and career opportunities for women before the war, poverty in their mother's family, hardships caused by the depression and the war. In the light of these comments, it is interesting to place in this context Foucault's (1980a) comments on what he called "the hysterization of women's bodies" during the medicalization of sex since the nineteenth century:

> a threefold process whereby the feminine body was analyzed—qualified and disqualified—as being thoroughly saturated with sexuality; whereby it was integrated into the sphere of medical practices, by reason of a pathology intrinsic to it; whereby, finally, it was placed in organic communication with the social body (whose regulated fecundity it was supposed to ensure), the family space (of which it had to be a substantial and functional element), and the life of children (which it produced and had to guarantee, by virtue of a biologico-moral responsibility lasting through the entire period of the children's education): the Mother, with her negative image of "nervous woman," constituted the most visible form of this hysterization. (p. 104)

By the 1960s, doctors had diagnosed a new variant of "hysteria" amongst middle-class American (as well as New Zealand, British, and other) housewives: "suburban neurosis" (Friedan, 1963). The promises of domestic bliss in the prosperous postwar environment seemed to many to be empty. Their careers put aside, isolated during the day in sprawling suburbs with few communal facilities, many middle-class housewives became clinically depressed and were prescribed the new "feel good"—and addictive—psychotropic drugs.

Their perceptions of their mothers as being unfulfilled fuelled a determination on the part of the majority of the women in this study to avoid becoming like them. For some this meant making the most of the educational, professional, and travel opportunities available during the postwar boom. All 12 women saw this as a major reason for their adoption of a feminist analysis in later life. Rejection of one's mother as a role model meant having to construct a new model of what a woman could or should be, and the various discourses of feminism offered creative possibilities. The determination to avoid the type of life lived by their mothers was a major incentive to some young girls to forgo early marriage and pregnancy. During the school years, virginity was the sexual strategy which was most likely to protect their personal and professional autonomy.

A second incentive for schoolgirls to remain virgins was the stigma against unmarried mothers. During the 1950s and 1960s there had been widespread public debate on the issue of juvenile delinquency (Department of Education, 1962; McDonald, 1978), which, in the case of girls, usually meant nonmarital sex.[2] Until 1972, there were no welfare benefits for single parents. Girls who became pregnant outside of marriage were often pressured by their parents into shotgun marriages, while others left home to hide their pregnancies from family and neighbors in homes for unmarried mothers or worked in domestic service on farms, giving their babies up for adoption soon after birth (Else, 1991). The stigma against unmarried mothers was so great that for some this acted as a strong deterrent on becoming heterosexually active.

Jill described her experience in a rural community where she was working after leaving school. She was saving her money in order to travel. At this stage of her life she did not have any clear ambitions for a career of her own, but believed that she would some day get married. Her horror at her mother's distress over an unexpected pregnancy when Jill was a child had left her with a determination not to have children of her own. At 19, she became involved in dating two boys, both of whom wanted to get engaged and have sex. Jill resisted:

> He'd go so far and not all the way. And that was really terrible. I
> think the strain of that is just fantastic. . . . I think that I had
> such a very good socialization from my parents that sex was bad.
> Wherever I got the message from, I got it loud and clear . . .
> there was this real terror of getting pregnant, because in country
> districts it's very looked down on, you're regarded as a slut. There
> has always been this antagonism in the country with solo mums
> [single moms].

The stigma against unmarried mothers was mentioned by all of the rural women in the study. Many of the urban women also mentioned it:

I remember my mother going to a meeting and hearing the ma-
tron of the Salvation Army home where they looked after the unmarried mums, Bethany. And she came back absolutely shocked
out of her mind recounting all these stories of all these young girls
and babies. I remember, every time I went out on a Friday night
to town, I got you know, like a 5-minute lecture about these girls
who got pregnant and she seemed really hung up about that for
about 8 weeks afterwards. My friends talked about that and said
how stupid it was and how hard it was to get contraceptives even
if they were thinking about, you know, going that far. But none
of them were, the boys or the girls, and this was in the senior
year. They got involved in sort of light petting, perhaps.

Although none of Pat's friends in the top streams had become pregnant, a number of girls in the lower streams had:

You see, we were in the top streams and there was no one in that
I can think of in our groups who got pregnant. . . . You were always hearing about, you know, the latest scandal of someone in
the lowest type of classes getting pregnant.

The academic girls' typification of lower stream girls as more likely to
fall pregnant was discussed in Chapter Two. It may have been that remaining a virgin was less important to some low-stream girls, since their future
careers did not require lengthy periods of training and early marriage could
release them from the drudgery of menial jobs. For the middle-class girl an
unplanned pregnancy could wreck not only her career opportunities, but
also her family's "marital strategies" (Donzelot, 1979) for her meeting and
marrying a professional husband.

Boys who were planning professional careers were also careful not to
"get caught." For example, Kelly became pregnant at 17. Her boyfriend
regarded her as an unsuitable mate and was prepared to lie to escape his
paternal responsibilities:

There was no talk of marriage, it wasn't that sort of relationship.
He wanted a career anyway, and I was a bit radical for him. I was
good company, but a little bit radical . . . there was a little bit of
wrangling because at this stage the boy didn't want me to di-
vulge. . . . He said "Don't tell anybody whose it is." He didn't
want to be implicated. The doctor said to me at this stage, "You
fool, you'll say that and then you'll want maintenance or some-

thing." Because then it was very difficult to get money out of any-body. I had to go to a lawyer.

For the academic girls, having a career meant delaying becoming too heavily involved sexually. While some viewed university primarily as a place to catch a husband, and could therefore afford to get serious in their student years, the major concern of *swots* (the 1960s slang equivalent of *nerd*) was academic success (Frame, 1983; McRobbie, 1978). Josephine described a subculture of swots in a girls school and their attitudes towards sexuality:

> They were all very much, pretty much the same as me, you know, involved in their work and rather despised boys actually. We were always above *those boys*. We didn't have much to do with men you see, it was mostly boys, the other schoolboys. And so, there-fore, we kind of thought they were greasy little grotty pimply crea-tures and couldn't stand them basically. . . . If anybody had a love bite on their neck it was kind of noticed and sometimes gig-gled about. But usually looked upon rather disdainfully.

Speaking of the girls in lower streams, she commented on the typifica-tions held of them by academic-stream girls. She noted that it was the habitus of the low-stream girls that gave the impression that they were more sexually active—their dress, their language, their jokes, and so forth:

> I don't actually know that they were all sexually active. I always had the impression that they were, because there were all these love bites and I don't actually really know whether they were all sexually active or not, but they used to talk, they used to make more crude jokes and it was just a stereotype that we had of them. But you see it's interesting because we never, as the top stream, never had anything to do with the rest of the school. We were totally unto ourselves, just self-sufficient and arrogant and kept to ourselves.

Lower stream girls did not necessarily envy or wish to emulate the swots, whom they often saw as headed for unglamorous spinsterhood (McRobbie, 1978). The curriculum in commercial (typing) streams empha-sized grooming and femininity as preparation for secretarial work (Taylor, 1984). One former "commercial girl" described the teachers of the academic stream as "stodgy" and offered the example of a science teacher who wore her hair "plainly done" and sported tweed skirts, plain blouses and flat-heeled shoes. At her school, she noted, while these teachers were unmarried, the commercial teachers were more likely to be married. Wearing high heels, tailored suits and with manicured finger-nails, they offered the girls an image of the sexually attractive perfect woman to which, as future secretaries, they were expected to aspire (Taylor, 1984). In contrast, the image of the intellectual woman was that of the "old maid"—to be an academic was to be asexual (Llewellyn, 1980; McRobbie, 1978). However, some academic stream girls from other schools described glamorous, well-traveled, highly qualified, and sexually experienced teachers who had inspired them to high intellectual, artistic, and romantic ambitions.

For some women, becoming sexually active was not a matter of choice; for some, loss of virginity was a result of sexual violence. Diane was raped and became pregnant at the age of 17 while in the sixth form; all she knew of her first experience of sexual intercourse was that she had gotten drunk at a teenage party and had "woken up lying in a pool of blood." When seven months pregnant, she gave up her job and moved to the North Island, where she lived in a home for unmarried mothers. As was the common pattern of the time, the baby was adopted (Else, 1991). At the time of the interviews, Diane had still not told her parents of these events:

> I chose to go overseas secretly and go through the whole pain of childbirth and stuff and finding my feet on my own in a strange place, broke, at the age of 19½ rather than deal with my mother being in on the situation. . . . I did not have the guts to stand up to them on it, you know, I am in such terror of her.

In later years, Diane analyzed her experience of rape and became active in helping other rape victims. While for some girls high academic, professional, or other aspirations helped to protect them from becoming involved in sexual relationships that would lead to early marriage, pregnancy, or both, for other girls it was family pressures that kept them from becoming sexually active, or, if they did, forced them to keep their sexual activities hidden from their parents. Although all 12 women had been brought up to believe that sex outside marriage was sinful and delinquent, by the time they were in their late teens to early twenties, not one of the women remained a virgin. All 12 experienced considerable tensions in their sex lives.

In order to understand the women's stories about the connections they made as young adults between their sexuality and feminism, it is necessary to outline briefly the feminist discourses available to them at the time.

FEMINIST WARRIORS IN THE SEXUAL REVOLUTION

The second wave of feminism crashed across the Western world in the late 1960s. Its history and discursive fragmentations—in academic and grassroots settings—were well documented at the time in many countries (Bunkle, 1979a, 1979b, 1979c, 1979d, 1980a; Eisenstein, 1981; Jaggar & Struhl, 1978).

Liberal feminists sought equality with men throughout the hierarchies of capitalism (Friedan, 1963). Because it spoke the language of policymaking, liberal feminism rapidly became the dominant (mainstream) feminist discourse and was incorporated into government and institutional policies on equal opportunities, antidiscrimination, and affirmative action (Middleton, 1993a). With respect to sexuality, liberal feminists sought freedom of choice in matters such as access to child care, contraception, and abortion so that women would be able to compete as individuals on equal terms with men. Woman's reproductive capacities were a potential obstacle to her equality, but the harnessing of the appropriate scientific technologies could make her more "like a man" if she chose to enter the contest. In the same way, she might freely choose the role of homemaker and mother, in which case affordable support services such as preschools should be provided.

While liberal feminism was premised on notions of disadvantage and discrimination within (an otherwise acceptable) socioeconomic system, radical feminism was premised on the concept of patriarchal oppression. The social system needed to be overthrown. Female sexuality was pivotal. For example, Shulamith Firestone (1979) argued that the parasitic institution of heterosexual "love" was the "pivot of modern women's oppression": "Men were thinking, writing and creating, because women were pouring their energy into those men; women are not creating culture because they are preoccupied with love" (p. 121). She argued that the sexual revolution of the 1960s and 1970s was yet another trap for women in that it brought no improvements for them, but instead proved to have great value for men. The discourse of the sexual revolution aimed to convince women that "the usual female games and demands were despicable, unfair, prudish, old-fashioned, puritanical and self-destructive" (pp. 135–136). This discourse offered men a wider market of sexually available females, while women were "disarmed of even the little protection they had so painfully acquired" (p. 135):

> Women today dare not make the old demands for fear of having a whole new vocabulary hurled at them: "Fucked up," "ballbreaker," "cockteaser," "a real drag," "a bad trip"—to be a "groovy chick" was the ideal. (p. 135)

Some of the more extreme strands of radical feminism advocated separatist strategies. Women should withdraw from all relations with men—economic, personal, and sexual. Lesbian separatism was a version of this movement (Johnson, 1973), although the sexual politics of many women with lesbian sexual orientations identified politically with other strands of feminism (Marxist, etc.), or with gay liberation rather than feminism.

Socialist, as well as radical, feminists of the time analyzed contradictions in postwar educated women's sexual lives. Marx's (1867/1976) writings had a great deal to say about the body. He exposed the exploitation of female and child labor in factories, and also showed how working-class women's unpaid work in the home—intimately concerning the body—had economic value and was therefore foundational in the oppressive capitalist class structure. Within the family women gave birth to children (biological reproduction); through their domestic labors they cared for the bodily needs of (male) workers and children (social reproduction); and also taught children the manners, habits, and demeanor necessary to performance during a working day (cultural reproduction). In addition, Engels (1891/1971) linked the oppression of women in the bourgeois family with private property and patriarchal systems of inheritance. Because these relied on a father's assurance of his paternity of his heirs, wives must be monogamous, although men could patronize prostitutes without disturbing the stability of this economic class and patriarchal order. The sexual double standard—good and bad women; monogamous wives and promiscuous whores—had a material base.

This analysis was used, for example, by Mary O'Brien (1982), who said that the contraceptive pill was changing the material base of human biological reproduction: It

> constitutes . . . a world-historical event . . . in that men and women are both in the position of having to mediate the separation of copulation and reproduction. The material and conceptual base of the "double standard" no longer exists, and women are currently exploring the ramifications of sexual freedom and control. (p. 110)

The contraceptive pill offered women the choice of voluntary infertility. Unlike the barrier methods of contraception, it promised spontaneity in sexual encounters. Many young single women embraced the pill, and some feminists joyously urged us all to go out and experiment, to explore, express, and glory in our newfound sexual freedom (Greer, 1971).

However, others (such as Firestone) argued that, instead of liberating us from the repressions of the double standard, the pill compounded our oppression in that the men of the 1960s conceptualized us as "playmates," "birds," or "chicks." Reproductive technology—articulated to the discursive regime of capitalist patriarchy—became a further means of female exploitation because of men's power over women and its control by commercial (capitalist) interests. As Heidi Hartmann (1981) commented:

> When children are seen as superfluous, women's sexuality for other than reproductive purposes is encouraged, but men will attempt to direct it toward satisfying male needs. (p. 36)

Socialist feminists saw the sexual revolution as a product of a society which was both capitalist and patriarchal. In the early 1970s magazines like *Playboy* were part of a rapidly growing pornography industry, and explicitly sexual images of women were increasingly used in advertising. Juliet Mitchell (1973) commented that

> illusorily offered the free and glorious expression of ourselves, it turned out to be only for a further alienation: turning ourselves into products which are then confiscated for use in a consumer society. (p. 142)

The pill was seen by some as making it difficult for many women to refuse to enter heterosexual relationships, since the fear of pregnancy had been almost removed. The permissive anarchy of the sexual revolution was constructed largely through the male-dominated commercial mass media, which presented images of women as playmates for men. According to socialist feminists such as Anne Foreman (1977) and Sheila Rowbotham (1973), this discourse alienated many women from their own sexuality.

Many women—both feminists and nonfeminists—rejected these critiques either wholly or in part and embraced in full the right to freedom of sexual expression and experimentation. Looking back on this period, Camille Paglia (1995) said, "I am a sixties free speech militant" (p. 50) and commented that

> the shrill melodrama of male oppressor/female victim came straight out of nickleodean strips of mustache-twirling villains and squealing maidens tied to train tracks. . . . What I call Betty Crocker feminism—a naively optimistic Polyannaish or Panglossian view of reality is behind much of this. (p. 25)

However, whatever view women took of the sexual revolution, it, in combination with the spectrum of feminisms of the time, widened the range of discursive positionings available to young women with respect to their bodies. There were fundamental contradictions between the sexual revolution's discourse of the "swinging chick" and the dominant discourse of heterosexual femininity (virginity until marriage followed by domesticity).

This compounded the experienced contradiction within liberalism itself—the dominant regime of truth in Western democracies. For, as argued in previous chapters, the allied discourses of heterosexual femininity and the liberal promise of equality of intellectual and professional opportunity were also contradictory (Eisenstein, 1981). These multiple and intersecting contradictions were profoundly lived out by the 12 women in my study. As feminists, they brought to bear on these the feminist discourses to which they had access and that offered theoretical interpretations for their personal dilemmas by linking these with wider social, political, cultural, and economic power relations.

SEXUAL STRATEGIES

Foucault did not do case studies of living people. Although he was fascinated with the archival records of individuals such as criminals and sexual "deviants" (e.g., Foucault, 1980c), his object of analysis was not the actual person, but the power relations which had brought the narrative into being: the nature of the authorities that had elicited the criminal's confession and its form (1977) and the regimes of truth that, for example, constructed the hermaphrodite as pathological (1980c). I need to go beyond Foucault if I am to theorize my case studies of how individual feminist women negotiated the contradictions, created meanings, and made choices with respect to their sexuality during the sexual revolution.

Feminist poststructuralists have made use of the idea of subject position (Davies, 1989; Gavey, 1992; A. Jones, 1993; Walkerdine, 1987; Weedon, 1987):

> Discourses make available positions for subjects to take up. These positions are in relation to other people. Like the subject and object of a sentence (and indeed expressed through such a grammar), women and men are placed in relation to each other through the meanings which a particular discourse makes available. (Hollway, 1984, p. 236)

For example, in Chapter One I gave the example of Nell Wilson who had experienced being positioned by a boy student as a "sex object" by having "bits of pornographic material" inserted in her roll book. The boy took up the subject position of consumer of sexist pornography and thereby positioned his teacher as object of the pornographic discourse (see also Walkerdine, 1987). However, within the discourse of teaching, *she*, as teacher, was positioned as subject and the *student* as object—she is the authority figure, and the boy, as a student, occupies a relatively powerless position. In this way we are all simultaneously, and fluidly, positioned in multiple, contradictory, and always shifting relations of power in relation to one another. I shall use this to help me explore how five of the women positioned themselves in relation to the contradictory discourses of the era of the sexual revolution.

By their late teens to early twenties all 12 women had experienced at least one sexual relationship. The patterns of sexual relationships they adopted may usefully be studied as strategies for dealing with their simultaneous and contradictory positionings in multiple and contradictory discourses and their "investments" in taking up or rejecting particular positions:

> By claiming that people have investments . . . in taking up certain positions in discourses, and consequently in relation to each other, I mean that there will be some satisfaction or pay-off or reward . . . for that person. The satisfaction may well be in contradiction with other resultant feelings. It is not necessarily conscious or rational. . . . An analysis which focuses on subjective positioning in discourses requires an account of the investment that a person has in taking up one position rather than another in a different discourse. Of course some discourses are more hegemonic and carry all the weight of social approval. (Hollway, 1984, p. 238)

To expand on her concept of investment, Hollway, like many contemporary feminists, draws on Lacanian psychoanalysis (Butler, 1993; Flax, 1990; Henriques, Hollway, Urwin, Venn, & Walkerdine, 1984; Grosz, 1989; Walkerdine, 1992). I am wary of this, for psychoanalysis is fundamentally—its premises and concepts are derived from—clinical therapeutic practice. Although I see the space here for a depth psychology, I shall retain my more sociological stance and stay well away from attempting to ascribe motivations, predispositions, or unconscious drives to my respondents. Instead, I shall coin the term *sexual strategy*. Whereas Foucault used the phrase *strategies of power* to signify vast social trends (the medicalization of sex, etc.), I shall use the term sexual strategy to refer to the path, or the pattern, of each woman's choice of sexual partners. I do not use the word *choice* as implying a rational decision, for there is nothing less rational than sexual passion! Four sexual strategies will be discussed here: lesbianism; overt nonmarital heterosexuality, including steady and casual relationship patterns, egalitarian marriage, and celibacy.

Coming Out as Lesbian

As a strategy, lesbianism offered the intellectual/professional woman the opportunity both to pursue a career and to satisfy her sexual needs; the contradiction between rational professional autonomy and sexual expression could be resolved through a rejection of patriarchal "femininity." However, in the 1960s the stigma against lesbianism remained great; male homosexuality remained illegal. Since the medicalization of sex in the nineteenth century, there had been what Foucault (1980a) described as "a psychiatrization of perverse pleasure":

> The sexual instinct was isolated as a separate biological and psychical instinct; a clinical analysis was made of all forms of anomalies by which it could be afflicted; it was assigned a role of normalization or pathologization with respect to all behavior; and finally, a corrective technology was sought for these anomalies. (p. 105)

During the 1950s, the mass hysteria engendered in the media by the Parker-Hume case (see Chapter Two) had exacerbated the pathologization of lesbians. The stigma against lesbianism in particular, and homosexuality in general, made the strategy of lesbianism difficult and stressful since it was unlikely to be accepted by families, peers, or colleagues (Glamuzina & Laurie, 1991).

The permissive discourse of the sexual revolution saw the emergence of gay rights groups in New Zealand, as lesbians and homosexual men sought legitimacy for their sexual preference. Perceiving the gay rights movement as being dominated by homosexual men seeking legal reform, some lesbian women began to form their own groups. Lesbians who positioned themselves as feminists also had to struggle for visibility and legitimacy within the women's movement, which was dominated by heterosexual women. A movement known as lesbian feminism was developed; it sought not merely to assert the right to an "alternative lifestyle," but also was defined as a form of resistance to the institution of patriarchy, or what Adrienne Rich (1980) called "compulsory heterosexuality." Several of the lesbian feminists in my study endorsed Rich's work as having been particularly relevant to their own lives.

Chris was the oldest sibling in a family of girls. From early childhood she had been physically active and good at sports. She did not enjoy the games and domestic tasks associated with "femininity" and strongly resisted pressures to make her "feminine." Although her father had encouraged her to do sports, he was ambivalent about her lack of what he thought of as femininity. Chris believed that her father had always wanted a son, yet when she behaved in a "boyish" way, she was punished for it. Chris's gender resistance became a source of conflict between her parents:

> I was getting into trouble with my parents for not wanting to do feminine things. . . . I kept being pressured especially by Dad to be inside and help my mother and that became a recurrent theme and by the time I was an adolescent it was a really bad source of conflict between me and my father. Meanwhile, I think he was really split because I think he wanted a boy, very much wanted a boy for his first baby. He didn't get it, so in order to be a father he didn't quite know what to do with this girl. And because I wanted to be outside and doing active things, one thing he did encourage me in was sport. . . . Meanwhile, he taught me how to dig the garden and grow vegetables, how to make concrete, how to make fences. I was hanging around when he was tinkering with the car. I spent a lot of time with Dad, far more time than I did with Mum. I liked doing that sort of thing but I didn't get approval for it.

Although pressured strongly to be feminine, Chris was cruelly punished when she behaved in a *heterosexually female* way. During her primary school years she suffered a brutal beating from her father for her first heterosexual experience, when she had become involved with a group of older boys and girls showing off their genital areas and "feeling each other up" in the bushes. The primary school principal had called in the police, her father had beaten her uncontrollably and made her swear not to tell her mother of this "disgrace." Chris observed that this event had taken place around the time of the Mazengarb Report (see Chapter Two). Here I am reminded of Foucault's (1980a) concept of "a pedagogization of children's sex":

> a double assertion that practically all children indulge or are prone to indulge in sexual activity; and that, being unwarranted, at the same time "natural" and "contrary to nature," this sexual activity posed physical and moral, individual and collective dangers. (p. 104)

During her secondary school years, Chris developed further strategies of resistance to the discourse of femininity (Connell et al., 1982). These included affecting a boyish mode of dress:

> I was a young dyke just quite obviously and I had my hair cut super-short and you just couldn't tell I wasn't an adolescent boy; ex-

cept for the fact that I had girls' gear on. Yet I never got victimized by my classmates. . . . I think I had a strong personality. I
succeeded at both classwork and sports and so nobody really victimized me. My classmates accepted me.

During her first years of secondary school, her lack of interest in boys
was seen as normal for academically and professionally ambitious girls in
the top stream in her city girls school:

We considered that we were meant to be there, to be at school,
that boys would come later. It was that era I think when still we
weren't expected to get involved with boys. If we ever did, it was
all incredibly ritual and formalized, there would be school dances
but only one a year and there would be the odd dancing class in
which Boys' College would be invited over or Boys' High would
be invited. But [on] no other occasions did we have anything to
do with boys; all the time we were encouraged to have to do with
girls. Like we had links to the other main girls school in the city, a
public school, and we would have sports days. We were very
sport oriented, and very academic oriented and boys came a distant third for most of the girls until about fifth form.

In her junior years, Chris's lesbian feelings were compatible with the
school's academic stream subculture. In fact, having crushes on older girls
or teachers was supportive of the school's emphasis on high academic and
sporting achievements in that they fostered strong identifications with successful academic, professional, and sporting women. Such crushes were
compatible with the long-term aims of academic-stream girls, who perceived overt heterosexuality as, at least temporarily, incompatible with
their vocational and educational goals:

Girls' College had this good tradition of dykes. It was seen as natural for girls to go through a stage or a phase in which they would
be in love with either teachers or other girls, and many of us
were. We talked about it to each other, and there were no problems. And crushes were quite normal. Like we talked about crushes, younger girls had crushes on older girls, it was expected.

However, by her senior year, Chris felt that the girls were coming
under greater pressure to dress and behave as "young ladies":

I was aware that I was going to be different—that I was unlikely
to fulfil many of the roles that were expected of me, that's how it

felt. My relatives who were always interested in such things, could say, "Oh well, you'll change. You'll find some nice man," or other stupid things, and I'd say, "I won't," and I was absolutely sure I never would. I didn't want to get older because it put me closer and closer to that age at which it would become apparent to everybody that I was not going to get married. I was not going to have babies and part of that was definitely to do with falling in love with girls.

At university, she became friendly with other lesbian women, was active in the gay rights movement, and experienced the separation of the women from the men's group as the differences in their collective experiences became apparent:

It was very much at that stage men and women, it was gay men and women, not lesbians at that point, together fighting various battles. . . . That's my only real contact with consciousness-raising groups. . . . It was in gay liberation. We went into things like having a lot of women in the room. We did actually split at that point. We recognized that there was a difference between the gay men's experience and the gay women's experience. Women would get together and talk about things, like I remember once where we talked about rape. I was absolutely horrified to discover that every women in the room, except for me and one other person, and there were about a dozen women in the room, had all been raped.

Chris's first encounter with feminism was hearing Germaine Greer (1971) speak during her New Zealand campus tour. She became personally involved with feminism in her midtwenties at university when she heard a talented older woman student being "put down" in class by the male lecturer for her feminist ideas:

This was the first time that anybody in any class that I'd been in mentioned a topic and said that it was feminist and I became aware that there were people around who were calling themselves some unusual name that I was not really familiar with. . . . This woman was in my class and she attempted to do a topic. . . . I remember at the time that it came up that the person taking it, the man taking the course, was pretty unsympathetic. . . . She was probably in her late thirties with a family and children, and she'd been around a lot and here she was—somebody whom he should have respected as a person and a student—coming up with something that was hers, clearly hers, which she was really involved in and I just remember getting this impression that it just wasn't treated as a topic which was acceptable, that was a real topic. I remember a lot of laughter. I just remember the attitude of the lecturer really struck me, that whereas others were coming up with things ,nobody seemed to question it and that was OK. Here was this really good student coming up with something and he was just saying, "Oh really do you think that's any use? And is this new funny feminist stuff?"

Chris immediately identified with this woman as an underdog; her own experiences of victimization, marginality, and discrimination as a lesbian and in other aspects of her life were evoked by this woman's treatment by the lecturer. Feminism addressed these feelings and experiences:

It was the feeling that either somebody was being treated differently without being laughed at or they were being victimized, something like that and it was the same feeling that I had and that was quite interesting . . . and I became interested instantly in feminism. What was this? Part of that is how I see myself in response to these situations . . . I am a person who because of the sort of characteristics I have don't easily fit into dominant structures . . . dominant teaching structures and dominant power structures in this society, being a lesbian and also being a working-class person. . . . The point at which I become aware that other people were being victimized, has had a lot to do with me and how I felt victimized, my feelings about myself.

At the time of the interview, Chris described her early feminism as addressing her experience of oppression as a lesbian in a heterosexist society that was premised on compulsory heterosexuality, her sense of alienation from gay men in the mixed-sex gay liberation movement, and her identification with the silencing and marginalizing of women's perspectives and feminist theory in academic settings. Marxism also attracted her, as she had a keen sense of marginality as a working-class girl and young woman when in academic settings. Although the dominant discourse of homophobia had meant painful struggles for acceptance, her creative sexual strategy allowed her to pursue an autonomous career.

"Losing" Virginity

A second sexual strategy was that of overt nonmarital heterosexuality. Living in apartments and hostels, many of us who were young in the late 1960s and early 1970s were free of our families' watchful supervision of our "moral welfare." Access to the new ideas of the "permissive era" and, possibly, the pill, as well as sheer loneliness, tempted many to experiment with our newfound freedom. Rejecting the lives of our mothers as undesirable examples, we sought to create new moral codes, new patterns of relationship. For many, the attractions of the contradictory positionings offered by the dominant discourse of virginity/domestic femininity and the increasingly influential ideas of the sexual revolution led to considerable stress. Brought up with a strict code of virginity-until-marriage, we experienced intense conflicts in relationships with parents.

For example, Mary Ingham (1982) researched the elaborate subterfuges of young women university students (all born in Britain in 1947) in hiding their sexual relationships from their parents—living with men, yet hiding their boyfriend's clothes when their parents visited their apartments. Similar scenarios were described by feminist novelists of the time (Alther, 1976; Piercy, 1983). If parents believed so strongly in the "virgin–whore" dichotomy, being open about one's love affairs could mean being stigmatized as whore by one's parents. This could mean loss of love, loss of family support. Many young women were unwilling to take that risk. Some found the stresses involved in maintaining a double life so intense that they failed their university courses, resuming their careers after marriage and children. The discourses of feminine heterosexuality and the liberal discourse of the rationally autonomous intellectual or professional were in conflict. Some chose to establish sexual and emotional "security" by marrying before concentrating on higher study or careers. Others—through rape or through "choice"—became heterosexually active outside marriage. Some lived an active single heterosexual lifestyle, and temporarily abandoned career plans, but resumed their education and training as adults. Sexuality, then intellectuality, dominated their lives in sequence.

Cathy had been academically successful at school and was taking a university degree in a male-dominated professional school, a path she had taken to please her parents. There she experienced discrimination against women by some male lecturers in a culture hostile to women:

> I spent a year at the school and that was just an unmitigated disaster from start to finish. It was actually very bad being a woman there in those days. In my year there were 70 guys and 3 females. One of the girls, we were all about 18, 19, then, left after 6

weeks. She decided she didn't like it and she wanted to do maths.
I should have done that but didn't. It was terribly hard. I left after
one year, the other girl stayed there the whole time, but she managed to deal with it. She was a very "twinset-and-pearl" sort of
dressing lady, she used to go along there in tweed skirts, twinsets
and pearls and looked like she was 40 and sit at the back and
never open her mouth. She had this protective ladylike cocoon
around her and that seemed to be how she survived.

Finding the conflict between her academic work and the desire for
sexual experimentation and emotional security too intense, Cathy focused
her energies on the latter, a strategy which resulted in her failing her university courses and dropping out of the program. Cathy described herself as

putting a hell of a lot more energy into my sex life and my emotional life than I ever did into my work and really university was
just a backdrop against which the dramas of my sex life were
played out. All sorts of things that were totally anathema to my
parents were played out.

She threw herself into student life, stimulated by the social and political
networks and activities of the late 1960s:

I just absolutely adored being at university. Floating around in the
coffee bars. There were demonstrations starting—the Vietnam
War. I just loved the whole thing. It was the beginning of breaking away from home.

However, she found aspects of student life lonely and worried a great
deal about finding a suitable "mate." She "lost her virginity" in her first
year. Her first experience of sexual intercourse was not pleasant. Cathy had
consented to this relationship because of loneliness and because she could
not think of adequate reasons to refuse. The discourse of the sexual revolution triumphed over the discourse of virginity into which her family and
schooling had positioned her:

I did not like him very much, but it was very nice not to be by
yourself the entire time. Anyway he wanted to go to bed with me
and I didn't particularly want to and I remember saying, "I want
to be a virgin for the man I marry," and he said to me, "Why?" I
thought, "Christ, I don't know." I said, "All right, I'll sleep with
you tomorrow." He got very excited, so that was it.

At this time, Cathy drifted into relationships, largely through fear of loneliness and a lack of a sense of direction in her education and career. She was frightened of becoming pregnant; at that time the pill was not available on her campus except on the black market and few doctors from the town would prescribe it for single women:

> It was absolutely insane, I feel quite weak at the knees when I think about it. For 10 months I was sleeping with him on and off. A lot of that time we were actually living together. For only 3 months out of that entire time was I on the pill. The rest of the time he used to try and remember to withdraw before he ejaculated. But of course it was pretty nondescript sex. On the other hand I felt that that was one of life's great mysteries that was no longer a great mystery. I would have just completely fucked my life if I'd got pregnant then. But you couldn't get the pill in those days. . . . It was just dreadful. If you knew a doctor who would give it to somebody that wasn't married, the word would go around like wildfire.

Cathy suffered intense conflict between her parents' view of sex outside marriage and the laissez-faire attitudes of her student subculture. She resolved this through resorting to subterfuge to maintain the pretence in the eyes of her parents that she was a "good girl." However, her sexual relationships gave her little pleasure. Lonely after a broken relationship, she had a series of one-night stands to avoid sleeping alone.

Rather than being primarily a place to obtain a degree, university was for Cathy a site for enacting her marital strategies. Cathy dropped out of university and took an office job. She later met a man whom she married, and had children. She stayed at home with her children when they were very young, then applied for teachers college. She became certified as a teacher and got her degree, with many *A*'s. Sexuality, then intellectuality/ professionality, had dominated her life in sequence:

> It was a matter of how much energy I had. My sex life and my love life was just far more important. I could never see the intellectual thing as being important then . . . there was no way I could have concentrated on work. I very much wanted a steady relationship with one person and most of my energy when I was young was directed at finding that. I don't think I could have ever succeeded at university without that. I feel so much different being at university or studying now because I've got that all sorted out.

Cathy has not been actively involved in feminist groups but espoused a liberal feminist philosophy, which she attributed to her perceptions of the difficulties that women faced in achieving equal political and professional opportunities. Her mother's and grandmother's difficulties in achieving professional success were described as particularly strong influences. Cathy's liberal feminist activism was directed at helping her daughters to achieve financial and personal autonomy and encouraging the girls she taught to take nontraditional subjects:

> What I can't believe is that anyone, any woman can say she is not a feminist. I think I'm a feminist because I want my daughters to be independent, choosing their own lives, not according to men — that their life choices are not limited because of, say, a relationship with a particular man or men in general. Starting from right back . . . my mother was basically brought up to think that she should really do what her husband said. There's no way that I would ever have been part of that. I accept that women in our generation . . . that did want to achieve academically had enormous struggles against their families and against what society said they should do. . . . My strongest value thing is justice. I have a very strong feel of justice. I think my feminism arises out of the fact that I think that women have been unjustly treated for generations and generations.

Getting Married

A third sexual strategy was marriage. The pressures on the girls of the 1960s to conform to the dictates of the dominant discourse of heterosexual marital femininity have been well documented in this book and elsewhere (Friedan, 1963). Foucault (1980a) framed this in terms of the broad social strategy of " socialization of procreative behavior," by which he meant:

> an economic socialization via all the incitements and restrictions, the "social" and fiscal measures brought to bear on the fertility of couples; a political socialization achieved through the "responsibilization" of couples with regard to the social body as a whole (which had to be limited or on the contrary reinvigorated), and a medical socialization carried out by attributing a pathogenic value—for the individual and the species—to birth-control practices. (p. 104)

By the end of World War II, the restrictions on access to birth control, on the grounds that it encouraged "loose" behavior (Tolerton, 1992), had been lifted for married women, although as late as the early 1970s, many doctors continued to refuse to prescribe the pill or to give contraceptive information or advice to single women on "moral" grounds.

Young women could avoid the conflict between the dominant ideology of virginity-until-marriage and their desire for sexual expression by getting married. During the 1950s and 1960s many women abandoned their education to do this (Friedan, 1963). For young women brought up with a strict code of conventional heterosexual morality, early marriage was a way of avoiding confrontations with parents. Cynthia had been brought up with strict religious principles. She commented that her peers in the church had not followed the trend at the time of openly living together, although some of them had furtive sexual relationships:

> There was somebody I would've very much like to have lived
> with. We bedded to a certain extent, but to have actually have
> *lived* together. You know, it would have just been so unspeakable
> in terms of our families. It would have been incredible. So most of
> us, we all went and got ourselves married.

Cynthia had always seen herself as having an independent career and had strong feelings against becoming financially or emotionally dependent on men. However, she had always taken it for granted that she would get married:

> There was always this sort of feeling . . . I knew nobody else like
> myself who didn't want to. I suppose I did want to sort of be
> "with somebody." But I knew nobody who'd decided purposely
> they weren't going to get married. Everybody I knew was getting
> married.

Cynthia said that she had gotten married to a man who "had been pestering me for ages" in order to have sex and companionship. Her husband was highly successful in his profession and shared her belief in the equality of the sexes. They planned to travel together and to delay having children, a decision which was seen as radical by others from their religious sect:

> The reason I agreed to marry him — he'd been pestering me for
> ages — was the fact that (a) we wouldn't be having any children
> for some years and (b) that we would be going overseas and there
> was no way I was going to give up that. . . . I felt I was quite radi-
> cal; at least, I was getting married and going on the pill and not

going to have children. Everybody else I knew was saving up for
their first house. And I thought, we thought, we were quite with
it; you know, we didn't even buy furniture before we got married.
We got married and then went away for a holiday. Then came
back and sort of vaguely looking for a flat, and we had $40 in the
bank and we went and spent it on a bit of furniture. And I
thought that was radical enough.

Cynthia and her husband travelled and, when they returned, had a
baby. Cynthia tried to remain in teaching, but due to the lack of child care
had to give up her job. Although she had by this stage read some feminist
literature, such as Greer's *The Female Eunuch*, she had not connected the
theory to her own experience. It was the experience of motherhood and the
irreconcilability of its demands with her career ambitions that led her to
make the connection. In the feminist jargon of the day, the "personal"
became "political":

There's this sort of separation between what you read and your
theory and practice anyway — it's very hard to get them together.
And, in many ways, it hadn't ever touched me, and it wasn't till I
had children that for the first time I suddenly realized what the
books, what feminism was about. . . . [It was] having to give up
my job. We kept delaying having children because I didn't want
to give up my job. I loved work and I knew there would be problems when I gave it up. We couldn't see any way around it. I tried
to get nursery care and find a child-care minder. I couldn't get any-
body suitable . . . and so I had to resign my position eventually.
And, you know, I was devastated.

Cynthia felt that her identity as an individual (her subject position as
rationally autonomous professional) was threatened by being financially
dependent on her husband:

I hated being financially dependent, and it wasn't as if I had a
mean husband. He would have given me anything. You know, he
used to bank an allowance for me. It was up to me what I did
with it, there were never any issues or anything. But I just felt
very uncomfortable being financially dependent.

Cynthia tackled this situation by finding work she could do at home to
earn some money of her own. After having her second child, she went to
university, child care being by then available on campus. After completing
her degree, she resumed her teaching career.

Sleeping Around

Three women, all victims of sexual abuse (rape, assault, or incest) described their patterns of sexual behavior in early adulthood as "promiscuous," while a fourth described a brief phase of one-night stands as a reaction to a broken love affair and the loneliness of sleeping alone. Two women who had left school at 15 and 17 fell into a pattern of sharing apartments and beds with a sequence of men. For these women sexuality triumphed over any intellectual or vocational aspirations they may have had. It was only when, as adults, they had established stable sexual relationships that they were able to take up their higher education and train for a teaching career.

Rachel was raped while still at school. Her home life was violent, and by the time she was in her senior years at secondary school, the situation had become intolerable. At the first opportunity, she ran away from home. Since her rapes she had become what she described as "promiscuous." Her creative strategy was to use her sexuality to support herself. Finding that her sexuality had economic value; she exchanged her domestic and sexual services for food and shelter:

> I'd just turned 16. I was doing well at school in my schoolwork, but my emotional behaviour, my emotional state was really terrible and I just couldn't stand it at home. So I went and I was living with these guys in this flat and I'd taken off in the middle of the night. I stayed there for about a week and I had no money. I used to clean up the house for them and they'd come back and I'd cook their meals and stuff. I guess I was being used. I was being used just as a housekeeper and a cook and to have sex on the sideline.

After being found by the police and returned home, Rachel ran away again. This time her mother refused to take her back, and this was the end of her schooling. Rachel's description of these events illustrated clearly how her sexuality was at this time her means of escape and survival. Sexuality dominated her life and intellectuality/professionality was temporarily abandoned. Throughout her troubled adolescence, Rachel had wanted and needed affection from her mother. She could not communicate with her at all about sexual matters. Her mother found out about Rachel's promiscuity. However, this did not lead to communication, but to further rejection:

> Mum found my diary when I was about 14, and I'd sort of listed all the guys that I'd been sleeping with and all sorts of things like that. And, in a way I was quite pleased that she had found it be-

cause she could see, she had to face up to talking about sex, but she didn't even face up to it then. She started telling me that I was a slut and all these names like this, and she just sort of kept yelling names at me and that was about it, that was all she said. She didn't really say anything much else at all.

Rachel became pregnant in her late teens and later married the baby's father. Like her own father, her husband was prone to violence and she was beaten by him on a number of occasions. She decided to resume her education and train for teaching as a means of establishing financial independence. Her husband did not support these efforts at first and Rachel had to resort to desperate measures to win his support. She gained strength from feminist women, also older students, in her teachers college class:

> I really started feeling confident in myself to start making sure that at home with my husband I was going to start being my own person. I found that the kids were the main hassle, the main drag, because to get to achieve my aim of becoming a person in my own right who had a right to do things, I had to leave the kids by themselves because he'd go out and refuse to look after the kids so I would say, "Right, now, I'm going out. You're not going to be responsible, then I'm not going to be responsible," so I'd just take off down the road or jump in the car and off I'd go and the kids'd be just left. And it happened on quite a few occasions. And it took about 2 or 3 months before he really realized I meant it, either he was going to start being just as responsible for them, or nobody was going to be responsible for them, and I felt really terribly guilty when I did it. I really did, I used to feel absolutely terrible. But then he started, he did start, taking on the responsibility that he'd never taken on before and the same thing happened with housework. I just refused to do it, I wouldn't do it. He kept saying, "Oh, God, this place is in a mess! What about doing the dishes?" And I'd say, "If you make a start, I'll come and help you," and it just carried on like that all the time. I just got, somehow got the courage to just start. I knew that I had my own money. This is the main thing, I think; if I left, I could support myself, and he knew it too and so he knew that if we wanted to stay together, it was going to have to start changing, everything was going to have to start changing, and, believe it or not, it did.

Rachel's life was dominated by sexuality, then intellectuality, in sequence. Because of her rape, the question of whether or not to remain a virgin did not arise. However, her sexual precocity had to remain hidden from her mother, and when it was discovered, led to rejection. In the mid-1980s Rachel became a talented schoolteacher who actively tackled the issue of sex-stereotyping in the classroom and worked closely with her pupils' parents in raising consciousness on the issues of sexism and racism.

Separatism and Celibacy

A fourth sexual strategy was celibacy. Remaining single has been a strategy of "career women" for generations. However, the "spinster" or "old maid" has often been a figure of fun, an object of pity. All of the women in this study were sexually experienced. While celibacy among women has often been seen as a sign of inadequacy, of being a failure or "left on the shelf," some 1970s feminists espoused a "new" celibacy, a voluntary withdrawal from sexual activity as a political statement and as a therapeutic process. This strategy was espoused for about a year by one of the women in this study. Identifying herself closely with other feminist women, she withdrew as much as possible from any relationships with men into a separatist, sexually celibate, lifestyle. Her term for this strategy was "political lesbianism" (Johnson, 1973) because it referred to a *deliberate* withdrawal from sexual relationships with men in order to explore with other women, through consciousness-raising, the nature and bases of women's sexual oppression and exploitation in a patriarchal society. *Political lesbians* were seen as lesbian separatists in all but the physical sense, since many associated almost exclusively with women in their domestic, educational, working, and recreational lives (Johnson, 1973; Rich, 1980).

Cora had had very painful experiences in her heterosexual relationships, which included rape, a teenage pregnancy, and a resulting estrangement from her parents. She had begun to attend university as an adult student and it was here that she first encountered feminist ideas. However, she had already developed an awareness of other forms of oppression, those of class and race, and had always expressed feminist sympathies after sensing her mother's frustration and unhappiness educationally and professionally. Cora had moved into a house with other feminist women, all of whom had experienced unhappy marriages and divorce. As a group they began, through consciousness-raising, reading, and their women's studies courses, to develop a collective analysis of their experiences of oppression:

> We had a lot of questions about the way that male/female relationships usually are. So I think that what we did then was get out of our sexuality, out of our bodies and with that motivation we got very much more into our heads and what followed was sev-

eral months of really intensive feminist theorizing. A great deal of sitting around talking and analyzing our childhood experiences, our grown-up experiences, our experiences and relationships and marriages. Every time we went out the door and had any kind of interaction in the outside world we would come back and analyze it in terms of feminist theory. . . . I think it was basically a consciousness-raising process. Some of us were doing women's studies courses at university. At that stage our courses didn't get very deeply into theory, although there was definitely input from there. I found it, and still find it, very hard to draw the line between personal life, political life, the education I receive, and the educational work that I'm doing—teaching others—my job, it's all very much bound up as part of the same process. So it's really hard for me to say if I was taking things back from those women's studies lectures and tutorials back to my household of women or if the flow was going the other way. I think it was actually going both ways. Specific books certainly, and specific feminist theorists, certainly had influence on us, but often it was indirectly.

Cora offered an interesting description of the way in which the ideas expounded by particular theorists became part of the intellectual currency of the entire group, a useful record of an educational process occurring outside formal educational institutions:

I remember a sort of turning point for me in that whole period was a particular conversation when one of the women I was closely involved with read *Lesbian Nation*, by Jill Johnston [1973] and talked about the theory of "heterosexism" which I had never come across before. It was something I had always known, it seemed, when it was described and we just sat and had this very long conversation.

Cora began to see the world in terms of the theory of heterosexism, or compulsory heterosexuality. She saw women as being physically maimed and deformed by the constricting clothing they wore to please men, women as shaped according to male desires and expectations:

Around this time if I was walking down the street, I would hardly notice the men at all. Later in the process the men seemed to me like alien creatures—a totally different species to women and I just didn't relate to them at all. At other times I would see men walking down the street with women, obviously heterosexual women, very much in the mode of women as adapted by newspaper advertisements, the media image of women, the very stereotyped image of how a woman should be. I'd see men walking down the street with women tottering on their high heels with their hair looking uncomfortable or wearing clothes that didn't look comfortable. And the men striding beside them, much more using their bodies, much more in their clothes and using body language, it would seem more comfortable and free and it seemed to me at that time that the women were absolutely captive. It seemed to me that they were less than human, less than the men.

Cora's intellectuality was focused on coming to understand her, and other women's, social conditioning for compulsory heterosexuality. Her sense of alienation from men and her growing sense of identification with other women led her to question her heterosexuality:

One of the first significant conversations we had, I said with great pain and humor, I think, about the trials of being a radical feminist heterosexual and just what that meant. An expression I used then and was thinking about the other day was that I had painted myself into a corner by having developed my ideas about male/female relationships in such a way that although I identified as heterosexual, I was finding it impossible to contemplate having sexual emotional relationships with men. The next stage was actually putting that to the test and going into a period of celibacy. In this period of celibacy, getting more and more into the theory, we began to identify ourselves as political lesbians because of being influenced particularly by theories such as that of Jill Johnston and heterosexism and so on, and I began to see that as a logical extension of radical feminist theory. I was celibate, increasingly alienated from men, increasingly attributing to the patriarchy all the problems of women and of ourselves, to such an extent that we had no desire to now, and perhaps ever, be having sexual emotional relationships with men. What friendships we had with men were becoming increasingly fragile; we had no desire to spend time with them.

Political celibacy provided Cora with a means of retreat from exploitative relationships with men. After about a year, the group split: some members came out as sexually active lesbians, while others resumed a pattern of heterosexuality.

DISCUSSION

These case studies have explored relationships between the feminist analyses and the sexual experiences of 12 teachers of the post–World War II generation. They reveal the complexities of the process that they went through in taking up positioning in the multiple, simultaneous, and contradictory discourses of the various feminisms and other movements for sexual liberation in the 1960s and 1970s. As Foucault (1980a) conceptualized it,

> Sexuality must not be thought of as a kind of natural given which power tries to hold in check, or as an obscure domain which knowledge tries gradually to uncover. It is the name that can be given to a historical construct: not a furtive reality that is difficult to grasp, but a great surface network in which the stimulation of bodies, the intensification of pleasures, the incitement to discourse, the formation of special knowledges, the strengthening of controls and resistances, are linked to one another, in accordance with a few major strategies of knowledge and power. (pp. 105–106)

Today in the late 1990s we are reaping the legacy of the personal conflicts, liberation movements, and political debates which erupted through the cracks and fissures of the sexual contradictions of this time. Although legal discriminations against sexual minorities have been largely removed, conservative oppositions to the sexual freedoms they fought for have mobilized, especially in the United States (Klatch, 1987). Questions of freedom of expression with respect to sexuality—around pornography and prostitution—have split the feminist movement (Paglia, 1995; Segal & McIntosh, 1992; Strossen, 1995). The demand for protection of women from sexual harassment has, some have said, led to excessive restrictions on freedom of expression for both sexes. Speaking of her 1960s generation, Camille Paglia (1995) writes, "We said to the colleges, 'Get out of our sex lives!' . . . Now today feminism is so stupid, it wants authority figures back into sex" (p. 242). In a manner unthinkable to sexual libertarians in the 1960s, some of today's feminists (Dworkin, 1981; McKinnon, 1989) have allied themselves with New Right religious conservatives to fight against pornography and prostitution. Separately and in concert these movements have wide implications for education (Fine, 1988; Sears, 1992b; Silin, 1995), as they question the free and open discussion of sexual matters in key educational settings—schools, universities, and cyberspace. It is to these matters that I shall now turn.

CHAPTER FOUR

Indecent Thoughts:
The Politics of Censorship

The sexual revolution was fought over freedoms to speak about sex, to create and to act out sexual fantasies, and to normalize sexualities which had up to that time been classified as deviant or pathological. Foucault (1980b) saw this as exemplary of the "productivity" of power. For, rather than being merely repressive of sex, the technologies of surveillance and discipline in families, schools, the medical profession, and so on, also gave form to desires:

> Sexuality, through thus becoming an object of analysis and concern, surveillance and control, engenders at the same time an intensification of each individual's desire, for, in and over his body. The body thus became the issue of a conflict between parents and children, the child and the instances of control. The revolt of the sexual body is the reverse effect of this encroachment. What is the response on the side of power? An economic (and perhaps also ideological) exploitation of eroticization, from sun-tan products to pornographic films. Responding precisely to the revolt of the body, we find a new mode of investment which presents itself no longer in the form of control by repression but that of control by stimulation. (pp. 56–57)

The commercial mass production of erotic magazines, films, and videotapes took off in the 1970s (Stoller, 1991). As commodities in the global capitalist marketplace, American, British, Scandinavian, and German pornographic[1] magazines and, later, videotapes began to flood down from the northern hemisphere into my part of the world—the South Pacific.

In March 1996 I was surfing the World Wide Web. On several home pages that I visited, there was a graphic with a blue ribbon—like the red ribbon people wear in support of AIDS sufferers. After a few minutes of pointing and clicking I found myself immersed in the Blue Ribbon Campaign for Online Freedom of Speech. I "visited" American senators and civil rights organizations, and eventually downloaded the document that had generated all this discussion within the United States and in cyberspace: a draft of the then-imminent Communications Decency Act of 1995. In the following weeks, debates over this American censorship bill also surfaced on satellite television and in my local print media. At that time New Zealand was also embroiled in debates over our own, similar, legislation.[2] Fearing prosecution, some providers of Internet access—including my own university—began voluntarily blocking off access to sexual material. Such censorship is done by screening out data on the basis of the name or descriptor of certain news groups or sites—such as all of the news groups that are subsumed under the header *alt.sex*. It is assumed that what goes on there—to use the terminology of the U.S. draft legislation—is "obscene, lewd, lascivious, filthy, or indecent."[3] While some of the material may include objectionable messages, say, from pedophilia "information" groups, it can also include the sharing of information about sexually transmitted diseases, or support for those with "sexual dysfunction." When blocking is done, however, on the basis of a single word, both the good and the bad are banned; and pedophiles can merely go underground and hide under a header like "trees" or "boots."

Whatever the fate of that U.S. draft legislation,[4] the issues it raised are broader ones. Nadine Strossen (1995), a leading U.S. lawyer,[5] has argued that

> the First Amendment's broadly phrased free speech guarantee—"Congress shall make no law . . . abridging the freedom of speech"—contains no exception for sexual expression. Nevertheless, the Supreme Court has consistently read such an exception into the First Amendment, allowing sexual speech to be restricted or even banned under circumstances in which it would not allow other types of speech to be limited. While American law is, overall, the most speech-protective in the world, it is far less protective of sexual speech than the law in some other countries. Our First Amendment jurisprudence, along with everything else in our culture . . . treats sex as a "special case." (p. 38)

Unlike the United States, many Western democracies impose statutory limitations on free speech with respect to sex and violence. New Zealand has a long, and some say at times repressive, tradition of censorship (Perry, 1965, 1980). What are the tensions between censorship and the freedoms promised by democracy? Censorship legislation empowers censorship authorities and courts to rule on the meaning of a word like *indecent*. What is involved in determining the meaning of such a word? And what are some implications of this for education as we increasingly seek information, knowledge, and communication with one another in cyberspace?

In Foucauldian terms, censorship statutes, case law, and censorship authorities are disciplinary apparatuses for the surveillance and regulation of language and visual images and can be studied within Foucault's framing of the broad disciplinary mechanisms of power-knowledge.

READING DIRTY BOOKS

From October 1987 until the end of 1993 I was one of five citizen members of New Zealand's Indecent Publications Tribunal, a statutory authority that, from 1963 to 1993, was charged by government with responsibility for the surveillance, monitoring, regulation, and classification of printed materials—books and magazines (Perry, 1965, 1980). Once a month, I flew to Wellington [New Zealand's capital] to participate in a hearing of the tribunal at the district court. In preparation for each hearing, I read between 100 and 300 magazines and several books. My work ended because the tribunal that employed me was abolished—along with the bodies that worked on films and videos[6]—with the passing of the Films, Videos and Publications Classification Act, 1993.

During my 6 years on the Indecent Publications Tribunal, people often asked me the following questions: Who were the people who got onto the tribunal and how were they selected? How were decisions about the classification of publications made? What, and whose, criteria were used as the basis or standards against which publications were judged? What or whose theoretical or political positions did these standards embody? Had these criteria or standards changed over time, and, if so, how and why did such changes come about? Did—and, if so, where and how—feminism come into the censorship process? What impact did reading so much pornographic material have on the censors and did we become "desensitized"? Would the new legislation be a change for the better?

This chapter addresses these questions by means of a chronological account of the changes in censorship criteria in which I participated during my term of office. I shall draw on this experience to raise two questions: What implications has such legislation for scholarship, research, and the arts in general and for feminist scholars, researchers, and artists in particular? And what can I draw from my local experience with the censorship of print media as a contribution to current international debates on the disciplining of speech in cyberspace?

As a former censor who is writing about censorship, my vantage point cannot be that of the traditional academic, who "stands outside" what s/he is studying (Middleton, 1993b; D. Smith, 1987, 1990). Mine is not, for example, the gaze of the scholar who dispassionately scans library databases in order to compile objective overviews of the literature. Neither is it the stance of the empirical researcher whose aim is to isolate and study the effects of pornography on individuals (e.g., Donnerstein, Lintz, & Penrod, 1987). It is not the viewpoint of the feminist activist who seeks to design a clear definition of pornography and to lobby for its implementation in policy. The radical feminist technique of "define it then ban it" was of little use to me (e.g., Dworkin, 1981; Kappeler, 1986; McKinnon, 1989). Similarly, neither was the extreme feminist libertarian view—the opposite extreme:

> We need *more* lust, not *less* lust! Feminism is totally out of sync with what is *needed* now. OK? We want *more* pornography, *better* pornography. Pornography everywhere! (Paglia, 1995, p. 259)

As I revisit my years on the tribunal and think about how they shaped my views on what is usually described as pornography, I am reminded of Foucault's (1980a) concept of the "specific intellectual":

> The intellectual is not the "bearer of universal values." Rather it's the person occupying a specific position—but whose specificity is linked, in a society like ours, to the general functioning of an apparatus of truth. (p. 132)

As social scientists we should, he says, see ourselves not as the "masters of truth and justice," but as always/already inside the regimes of truth—the apparatuses of disciplinary power that are our object of study. As both feminist academic and censor, I was positioned as such a specific intellectual. The raw ingredients for this chapter came at me during my 6-year term. They included the various kinds of texts that were brought before the tribunal for consideration during my time of service and the conversations and other forms of human interactions in which I participated in the course of the tribunal's processes.

The tribunal's hearings took the form of courtroom dramas. We five members sat in judgment in a row behind a bench. Publications were submitted and defended by importers, distributors, retailers, and consumers. Community groups, customs officials, medical and other professionals made submissions or were called in to give evidence as expert witnesses. Every shade of community opinion and every variant of sexual preference and taste was played out, attacked and defended, before our eyes. Cloaked comic-book readers, sadomasochists of all shades of sexual orientation, lawyers in dark suits, the leaders of the conservative Society for the Promotion of Community Standards—these were just a few of the protagonists in the hearings in which I participated.

I can explain the nature of my data by grouping them into four categories. First, were the legal-rational criteria—the judicial discourse which structured our decision-making process—as laid down by Parliament in statutes and as established over time by the tribunal itself in its written decisions (precedents or case law) and in its resulting guidelines and policies. Second, there was the evidence that was brought before the tribunal by expert witnesses. The tribunal's hearings were open to the public, and submissions and evidence came before us in oral, written, and sometimes visual or tape-recorded form. Third, there were the potentially "indecent" texts themselves—books, magazines, and occasionally sound recordings. My work as a tribunal member was intertextual in that it involved reading the texts submitted to us (potentially indecent books, magazines, and sound recordings) and using other texts (statutes, prior decisions, guidelines or policies, and evidence from expert witnesses) as tools in the analysis and classification of the submitted texts.

All of these were discussed and argued through among ourselves during the meetings that were held after each public hearing. These conversations were the forums in which each decision was collectively made. The experiences and perspectives of each of the members—biographical, cultural, professional, and generational—were constitutive of our collective decisions. Despite the diversity of backgrounds of the tribunal members, it was only occasionally that we were unable to agree and, on only three out of thousands of decisions, did I disagree strongly enough with the other members about the classification of a publication to write a minority decision on it.

The narrative that I construct in this chapter is not based on other people's books or on disembodied ideas, but is rooted in all dimensions of my experience. Different tribunal members would no doubt write very different stories about the same events or select different events as being of greatest importance. In the spirit of postmodern writing, I shall identify some of the multiple influences and processes of my own theory construction by weaving a "theoretical autobiography" (an account of the development of my own theorizing) through a broader textual score of narratives about the wider discursive shifts within which my ideas about feminism and censorship have come to form. This broader context includes changes in the law, changes in the membership of the tribunal, changes in the tests of indecency (criteria or policies) that were written and applied by the tribunal, changes in the nature of the publications submitted, and changes in the intellectual and conceptual resources available to us.

A CENSOR'S APPRENTICESHIP

In the spring of 1986 I was on sabbatical from my job as a senior lecturer in education at the University of Waikato, and was based at La

Trobe University in Melbourne. I was somewhat astonished to receive a message from Bill Dillon, who was my local Labour member of Parliament. There was a vacancy on the Indecent Publications Tribunal and the minister of justice, Dr. Geoffrey Palmer, was calling for nominations. Would I be willing to have my name put forward for his consideration? It would involve a 5-year term.

The idea both interested and frightened me. As a professional academic, a wide reader, a lover of the arts, and as someone with a passion for the unconventional, I had a fear of censorship as an apparatus of the state. I'd had little contact with, or interest in, pornography, but, as I considered taking up this opportunity, three stark and conflicting encounters with it immediately sprang into my consciousness. I shall briefly describe these because they explain the nature of some of the perspectives I brought with me to the job and provide a baseline for an account of how my thinking developed and changed as a result of my experiences on the tribunal.

I had begun to discover feminism (in its late-1960s guise as "women's lib") towards the end of my student days. My version of women's lib fused two sets of interrelated ideas which were in the air around me. One was what we would now call the discourse of liberal feminism—along with my flatmates I had read Betty Friedan (1963) and Germaine Greer (1971), regularly purchased feminist magazines, and followed in the press the antics and statements of feminist groups. Women could—and should—do anything that men could do in the workplace and in private life. This resurgence of liberal feminism coincided with the sexual revolution. When *Playboy* appeared on the scene I thought little of it, seeing it as a celebration of the female body and of sensuality in general (Paglia, 1995). I rather envied the models for their lack of inhibition. The outcry by conservative groups such as the Society for the Protection of Community Standards seemed to me nothing more than prudery and a threat to the liberation we young women seemed to be about to attain. Like Camille Paglia (1995), I would have described myself then as

> a Sixties free speech militant. As part of our rebellion, we middle-class girls flung round the raunchiest four-letter words we could find: we were trying to shatter the code of gentility, delicacy, and prudery that had imprisoned respectable women since the rise of the bourgeoisie after the industrial revolution. (p. 50)

This view was challenged in the early 1970s as I backpacked through Scandinavia. I Youth-hosteled where the hostels happened to be, and in one case—Amsterdam, I think—they were in the middle of the red-light district. Scantily clad women exposed their wares in shop windows. Live sex-shows were advertised on billboards—as casually as if the "product" were fish and chips. I was fascinated. Out of curiosity, I ventured into one of the adults-only magazine shops. There, displayed among the "adult" magazines were pictures of naked pubescent girls inserting candles and other objects into their vaginas. I still remember feeling sick. The young man who worked in the shop was looking at me curiously—I assumed because I was obviously a foreign tourist and because women didn't often venture in. I asked him where the children came from. "From North Africa," he said. Third World children exploited and degraded to gratify the fantasies of European pedophiles. From that moment I believed that there were circumstances in which censorship was necessary. Even the most hardened libertarians, including Foucault (Macey, 1995, p. 375), usually draw the line at kiddie-porn.

My third experience was 20 years later—at a large women's forum that was organized by the Labour government as a part of the setting up of the Ministry of Women's Affairs. Hundreds of local women attended this forum. There were feminists of all persuasions, most of whom—like me—were there to support the founding of the ministry. Local fundamentalist churches had mobilized a large contingent of antifeminist women who opposed the ministry as the product of a feminist plot to undermine the family and God-given gender roles (Klatch, 1987). Many of the workshops seethed with conflict between these two factions. By comparison, the workshop I had been asked to facilitate was an oasis of calm and consensus. Feminists and antifeminists from both ends of their various political spectra agreed with one another. I had been asked to chair the workshop on pornography. Using arguments similar to those of North American activists such as Andrea Dworkin (1981) and Catherine McKinnon (1989) these New Zealand radical feminists and Christian conservatives saw pornography as bad, as degrading to women, and as something which should be banned: "Pornography is an industry that mass produces sexual intrusion on, access to, possession and use of women by and for men for profit" (McKinnon, 1989, p. 195).

These experiences positioned me variously within the political and theoretical discourses concerning pornography and censorship. Many literature reviews of these positions have been written (Cheyne & Ryan, 1989; Jaggar, 1993; Morris, Haines, & Shallcrass, 1989; Segal & MacIntosh, 1992). While there are some differences in terminology and categorization of perspectives, most of the literature reviewers agree on the broad parameters of the more influential discourses on pornography and censorship. Libertarians prioritize the rights of the individual to freedom of expression, including sexual expression (Stoller, 1991). Basing their analysis on a bifurcation, or split, between public and private life, libertarians argue that the voyeuristic eyes of the state have no place in the bedroom, although many make some exceptions, such as in the case of child pornography or eroticizations of nonconsensual sexual violence. My inclination—as a young woman who had lived through the sexual revolution—was toward this perspective. However, my encounter with child pornography in Scandinavia had convinced me of the desirability of banning exploitative material. Moralist (or social conservative) discourses, such as those of some religious fundamentalists, saw the depiction of sexuality outside the bounds of marriage as immoral and as justifying prohibition by the state (Ryan, 1988). While I did not myself share that position, I believed in people's rights to their religious beliefs and to freedom from involuntary exposure to the kinds of sexually explicit materials that they found offensive. This meant that I supported controls on the public display of materials that were found to be not potentially harmful to all adults but that were offensive to many.

Feminist discourses have varied. Some veer towards the moralist or procensorship view, although for different reasons from those advanced by moralists. While the moralists (or social conservatives) see sex outside marriage as immoral and its depiction as undermining God-given gender roles within marriage (Klatch, 1987; Openshaw, 1983), procensorship feminists see pornography as exploitative and as denigrating of women, and its prohibition as a major battle in the eradication of sexism, of which traditional gender roles are manifestations (e.g., Women Against Pornography, 1989). For some (e.g., Dworkin, 1981; McKinnon, 1989) heterosexual intercourse itself is violent and unequal and therefore denigrating of women:

> What is sexual about pornography is what is unequal about social life. . . .
> Inequality is what is sexualized through pornography, it is what is sexual
> about it. The more unequal, the more sexual. (McKinnon, 1989, p. 143)

On the basis of my own sexual experiences, I did not share this view. Other feminists adopt a more libertarian stance (e.g., Cheyne & Ryan, 1989; Jaggar, 1993; Paglia, 1995; Segal & MacIntosh, 1992; Strossen, 1995). They express concern about prohibition as a technique; caution that feminists, too, might need and wish to create their own erotica; and that in procensorship regimes the erotic representations of sexual minorities (such as lesbian sadomasochists) are among the first to be prohibited. They also point out that the banning of pornography by some women has serious implications for the working conditions of other women, this being a concern because, as in the case of prostitution, most of the workers in the industry are women (Ronai, 1992; Stoller, 1991). Feminists should work to support sex workers in achieving safe working conditions rather than drive them further underground (Hanson, 1996; Jordan, 1991; McLeod,

1982). As someone whose thinking was strongly influenced by Marxism and socialist feminism, I had sympathy with this analysis.

Feminist sex workers have claimed that their right to work in the sex industry is a matter of freedom of choice. Far from being passive victims of patriarchal oppression, they see their sensuality as giving them "power over" men (Hanson, 1996; Paglia, 1995; Ronai, 1992). Nina Hartley—a U.S. porn star and business woman—explained:

> I grew up in Berkeley, the home of radical feminism, antisexism, and anti-objectification. I fit into that real well. But I was different inside. I was turned on by reading pornography since I first got my hands on it. I loved reading _Playboy_. I loved reading the _[Penthouse] Forum_. (Stoller, 1991, p. 140)

The voices of these women also influenced me.

A TESTING TIME: STARTING WORK

I accepted the nomination and some months later I was advised that I had been selected by the minister of justice to fill the vacancy on the tribunal. Early in 1987, three huge cardboard boxes full of magazines were delivered by courier to my front door. How should I read them? By what, or whose, criteria should they be judged? First, I turned to the legislation under which the tribunal had been set up—The Indecent Publications Act of 1963. Words like _pornography_ did not appear in the act. I would not be involved in defining or making decisions about pornography. The concept with which I would have to grapple would be "indecency"—which seemed rather quaint and archaic. In the words of the statute,

> "indecent" includes describing, depicting, expressing, or otherwise dealing with matters of sex, horror, crime, cruelty, or violence in a manner that is injurious to the public good. (Indecent Publications Act, 1963, S2)

In determining whether or not a publication was indecent, tribunal members were required (Section 11) to take the following into consideration:

(a) The dominant effect of the book or sound recording as a whole:

(b) The literary or artistic merit, or the medical, legal, political, social, or scientific character or importance of the book or sound recording:

(c) The persons, classes or persons, or age groups to or amongst whom the book or sound recording is or is intended or is likely to be published, heard, distributed, sold, exhibited, played, given, sent, or delivered:

(d) The price at which the book or sound recording sells or is intended to be sold.

(e) Whether any person is likely to be corrupted by reading the book or hearing the sound recording and whether other persons are likely to benefit therefrom:

(f) Whether the book or the sound recording displays an honest purpose and an honest thread of thought or whether it is merely camouflage designed to render acceptable any indecent parts of the book or sound recording.

I knew little about law. However, the juridical discourse which would direct and constrain my decision making—and the rules for the composition, procedures, and conduct of the body to which I had been appointed—had been established by Parliament by means of law and I would have to learn how to interpret and apply statutory criteria to the task of censorship. As a sociologist and as someone with an interest in politics, I understood that legislation concerning censorship results from (among other things) dynamics within and between community pressure groups, political parties, elected politicians, commercial interests (such as those in the magazine importing, distribution, and retailing business), and legal draftspersons. The concepts and wording of such legislation would embody elements of the thinking and sociohistorical contexts of those who produced it. For example, concepts such as indecency and corruption had an early-1960s feel to them. As outlined below, during 6 years of office, the passing of additional new civil rights legislation was to have an impact upon the tribunal's work, for example, the Homosexual Law Reform Act, 1986 and the Bill of Rights Act, 1990. As we grappled with both the 1960s and the more recent legislation, we were to find contradictions, anomalies, and inconsistencies between them.

Nine years later I don't remember much about that first box of books. I read them. I read the act. Then, confused, I went to Wellington for my first tribunal hearing. I was early. Judge Kearney, the chairperson, was friendly and jovial. Over a cup of tea, he explained to me that it was up to us as experts to determine questions such as: What is the public good and what would constitute injury to it? What is the significance of the "manner of depiction" in the determination of indecency? As tribunal members we were reading hundreds of publications before each meeting. He explained that to help us classify each publication we needed more specific rules of thumb, or recipes, than the statute on its own. On the basis of its own precedents, or past decisions, the tribunal had established short tests of indecency. The policy or guidelines under which the tribunal was then working had been established during the early 1980s in decisions with respect to several issues of the American edition of *Penthouse*. The tribunal had been particularly concerned about a still from the Fellini movie *Caligula* depicting a Roman orgy that included pseudolesbian scenes (sexual activities between women for the purposes of male voyeuristic gratification), bestiality, explicit sexual acts between groups of people, incest and sadomasochism.[7] This magazine, and others like it, had been banned, and a "test of indecency," which was to become known as the tripartite test, had been developed. It was important to have such a test because it enabled customs officials, and others who were screening publications at their point of entry into the country, to make judgments as to whether or not publications should be submitted for classification. This test was as follows:

1. Scenarios involving more than two models, and in which sex and violence and intimacy along with, or wihout, deviant aspects of sex are depicted among the models;
2. Multiple model scenes which depict lesbian acts;
3. Heterosexual scenarios in which there is a high degree of intimacy (e.g., fellatio or cunnilingus or intercourse) depicted in the couple's actions.

In addition, erotic depictions of sexual acts that were illegal—male homosexual acts, sex with children, and incest—were banned (unless an exception were made in the case of a publication which was deemed to be of artistic, literary, scientific, or scholarly merit). At the time I came onto the tribunal, all photographic depictions of actual or simulated sexual connections (oral, anal, or vaginal intercourse, cunnilingus or fellatio) were being banned.

Being on the tribunal created close bonds between its five members. There was a lot of laughter. Because there were five members and each member's usual term of appointment was for 5 years, one member would retire and a new one be appointed every year. This ensured that fresh perspectives were continually being brought to the group. The statutory requirements for the tribunal's composition were as follows:

(2) The tribunal shall consist of—
   (a) A barrister or solicitor of the High Court of not less than 7 years' practice, whether or not he holds or has held any judicial office, who shall be the Chairman of the tribunal:
   (b) Four other members of whom at least 2 shall have special qualifications in the field of literature or education. (Indecent Publications Act, 1963, S3)

At the time of my appointment, Judge Kearney chaired the tribunal, the award-winning novelist Keri Hulme[8] was the "expert in literature"; and the other members were a feminist criminologist, a city recreation officer, and myself.

Although I felt repelled by much of the material I had to read, I was fascinated by the experience of working with law, took pleasure in the company and ideas of the other tribunal members, and enjoyed the stimulation of the hearings. In some of my academic writing I began to explore tensions and contradictions between my emotional responses to the publications, my feminist and sociological theories, and the legal-rational criteria that I was required to apply to their classification (Middleton, 1988a; 1993b; 1994). However, while I gained intellectual, political, and personal satisfaction from the work, from the beginning I felt uncomfortable with aspects of the tripartite test. While I had no difficulty with the banning of materials that exploited children for the sexual gratification of adults, I could see no reason for the banning of photographic representations of consenting adults engaging in sexual activities. My gut reaction was that the test sometimes screened out the wrong materials.

To me a photograph of a single female model spreading her legs and offering her vagina to the male viewer seemed more demeaning than a photograph of a couple engaging in consensual sex. However, just before I came onto the tribunal, an appeal judge[9] had ruled that the tribunal could not use in the classification or publications concepts such as "demeaning," "denigrating," or "dehumanizing," such as those advocated in the McKinnon-Dworkin campaign in Canada and the United States, as in their following statement:

> The mass production of pornography universalizes the violation of the women in it, spreading it to all women, who are then exploited, used, abused and reduced as a result of men's consumption of it. (McKinnon, 1989, p. 201)

It was, the judge argued, a logical fallacy to argue that a photographic or textual representation of one woman demeaned all women. If the model herself had consented to the depiction, other women had no grounds for complaint. The legal-rational discourse in New Zealand was individualist.

During my first years of service there were several important changes in the legal parameters in which we were working. At the time I took up my position, the Homosexual Law Reform Act of 1986 had just come into effect, and this meant that gay men's publications were no longer illegal. While staying within the policy laid down by the Tripartite Test, the tribunal adopted a policy of having a single standard for gay and for heterosexual publications. For a time we were flooded with gay men's erotica as the importers remedied the gap in the market brought about by the prohibitions of the past. However, as in the case of heterosexual publications, only those magazines which depicted single models or multiple models who were not engaging in sexual activity were passed. Any depictions of sexual activity were banned.

On one occasion in 1987, Keri Hulme and I dissented from the majority decision and each wrote a minority decision. The book concerned was a 1972 gay men's sex manual called *Men Loving Men* (Decision 29/87). The majority decision was to declare this text "unconditionally indecent" (i.e., to ban it) on the grounds that it did not contain information about AIDS and did not sufficiently condemn the use of illegal drugs as sexual stimulants. In the course of writing my minority decision on this text (which was resubmitted and passed by the tribunal in 1993), I began to articulate my own position on the regulation and prohibition of sexually explicit material:

> Current notions of equity require that minority groups can see themselves reflected in the literature they read, and that their needs and rights are taken into account. Until the passing of the Homosexual Law Reform Act, homosexuals were subjected to the prohibition of both their sexual activities and much of their written history and culture. As an early publication emerging from within the gay rights movement, this book has considerable historical and cultural significance, not only for the gay community, but for members of the wider public concerned with knowledge about human history, sexuality, societies and cultures. (Minority Decision 29/87)

My academic work—in women's education, biculturalism and multiculturalism, and sociological theory—was primarily concerned with questions of equality and equity. The Tripartite Test seemed to screen out some materials that could be seen in terms of the rights of sexual minorities to sexual expression—in Foucault's (1980b) terms as the "underside and limit of power" (p. 138), and as part of "an insurrection of subjugated knowledges" (p. 81).

THE PENTHOUSE GUIDELINES

During my term of office, the tripartite test became increasingly unworkable. This reflected changes in the membership of the tribunal, shifts in community thinking, and changes in the nature of the publications being produced and imported. I became a participant in the creation and drafting of a new test of indecency that was popularly known as the *Penthouse Guidelines.*

By 1990 Judge Kearney and one other member had completed their terms of office. There were three members who remained from my time of joining the tribunal—including the writer Keri Hulme and myself. The tribunal had gained a new chair—Peter Cartwright, who had a strong background in civil liberties. The other new appointment was Bill Hastings, a senior lecturer in law at Victoria University, who also worked with the Video Classification Authority. There was general agreement among the members that the guidelines within which we working were no longer effective. For example, sexual explicitness did not in itself seem relevant as a basis for banning publications. The lawyers on the tribunal explained that, if we were to change the tribunal's guidelines and policies, we would need a test case in which specific erotic and explicit materials could be scrutinized in depth with the help of expert witnesses. There must be good reasons for such a shift in policy.

Penthouse International were willing and able to undertake an extensive (and expensive) defence of the American edition of *Penthouse*, several issues of which had previously been banned (i.e., classified as "unconditionally indecent"). Penthouse was of strategic importance because it had been largely upon readings of earlier issues of American *Penthouse* that the Tripartite Test itself had been formulated. Although the Australian edition of *Penthouse* was widely available (with an age restriction) in New Zealand, the American edition was different because each issue included a sequence of photographs showing some degree of sexual interaction between two models. The hearing took days. Both Penthouse and the tribunal (through the Crown Law Office) called in and cross-examined expert witnesses. Community groups made submissions. It was extraordinarily exciting. Among those who gave oral evidence or submissions were: a chief inspector of police; a professor of psychological medicine; two renowned American researchers into the effects of pornography on male behavior and attitudes; and a psychologist from an American seminary who appeared in support of the Society for the Promotion of Community Standards. In addition, there were written submissions and affidavits. In brief, we concluded that

> the gist of this evidence, very simply put, is that purely sexual depictions are not harmful per se; it is only when coercion or violence is combined with a sexual depiction that the depiction, according to some studies, could be harmful. (Decision 4/91, p. 37)

The process of doing the preliminary reading of hundreds of pages of submissions, of hearing the evidence, discussing it, and drafting, writing, and finalizing the decisions took many weeks. All this work resulted in new guidelines, a new "test of indecency," which we wrote in the decision and which guided our work until the tribunal's demise:

1. Depictions of violence, sexual violence, paedophilia, necrophilia, coprophilia, urolagnia and bestiality, which are not treated seriously and are intended as sexual stimuli are indecent; By "seriously" we mean a scholarly, literary, artistic or scientific work.
2. Depictions of sexual activity which demean or treat as inherently inferior or unequal any person or group of persons, which are not serious treatments and which are intended as sexual stimuli, are indecent (by way of example, this would include magazines the dominant content of which is the close-up depiction of genitalia or other body parts, and other depictions which reduce a person to her or his sexual parts);
3. Depictions of individuals or sexual activity which do not fall into the above categories are conditionally indecent or not indecent, depending on our application of the factors in s.11 (in this regard we emphasise matters of distribution) and the definition of indecency in s.2.[10]

I was proud of having contributed to the formulation and the writing of these guidelines. They were controversial. Religious conservatives publicly denounced our abandonment of the Tripartite Test, petitioned members of Parliament to legislate to bring it back and to fire the members of the tribunal. A conservative Catholic newspaper condemned the decision on the grounds that it leaned toward the views of liberals, feminists, and male academics: "The general public is not concerned only about extreme deviancy, violence, child abuse and the demeaning of women. . . . a lot of people are opposed to treating sexual acts of any kind as a subject for public display and commercial profit" (Moynihan, 1992b, p. 12). Readers were urged that with new legislation in the wind, "now is the time for the silent majority to let the authorities know what community standards are" (p. 12). While conservative groups were militantly opposed to the liberality of the new guidelines, feminist groups remained strangely silent.

I felt comfortable with the Penthouse guidelines up until the time my work finished, although the second guideline (to "demean or treat as inherently inferior or unequal any person or group of persons") proved particularly difficult to implement. It was often there that the rather blurry line was drawn between what was declared "unconditionally indecent" (banned) or given a "sex shops only" restricted age classification. The issue was usually not what was being depicted, but its manner of depiction. I can best explain this by means of an example.

In July 1993 I was reading through several boxes of "dirty books" in preparation for one of the final hearings of the tribunal. Most of the magazines in that set of boxes showed heterosexual or gay couples or threesomes engaging in explicit sexual activities. What concerned us as censors was not so much the showing of these acts (even though some may have offended our own personal morality) but whether they violated our second guideline, in other words, whether they were intended as sexual stimuli and "demeaned or treated as inherently inferior or unequal any person or group of persons." (Censor's warning: Those readers who are likely to feel upset by strong language and violent sexual images should not read the following three paragraphs.)

One of the magazines in those boxes was called *Asian Fuck Toys.* There were two "stories" (captioned photo sequences) in the magazine. I shall describe the second story, which was entitled "Su-Linn's Double Date." The narrative consisted of full-page color glossy photographs (presumably stills from a videotape), each of which was accompanied by a brief caption. On the first page, two large white men entered a room and approached the rear end of a small Asian woman, who was lifting her very short skirt and baring her bottom at them. There were no verbal introductions or greetings:

> Su-Linn was sure a hot number! It didn't take us long to play with her tits and suck her asshole. The afternoon had just begun and I was hot and bothered already!
>
> Sam couldn't stop licking her ass. It was the smoothest, silkiest ass he'd ever seen.

That was the only photograph that showed the female model's entire body and face. From the second photograph onward, all that was seen of her was her backside — with her anus and vagina being penetrated simultaneously by the men's penises which, because of the angle of the camera, seemed huge. There was only one other photograph which included the woman's face — a close-up of two penises in her mouth: "She put our peckers in her mouth and sucked 'til we were ready to burst!" The narrative constructed the woman as nothing more than a piece of meat — inert. She did not move, speak, cry out, or react in any way — in short, she was not depicted as human. The men were portrayed as all-powerful rapists who were conscious only of their own gratification and oblivious to what must have been agony for the woman:

> It was just too much for us. We both wanted her now. All I could think of was my wet dick was so slick with juices that I kept shov-

ing it harder and harder into her asshole while Sam was thrusting his prick into her pussy.

The action was moving along—faster and faster. I could feel the juices getting ready to explode from within me. Sam and I were getting a real workout.

I pumped and pumped and, finally, felt the oozing cum overflow. I pulled out so I could watch my cum flow over her ass cheeks. What a sight! Now, we can begin again!

The sequence also illustrated an extreme form of sexist racism (or racist sexism) with its concluding statement: "I couldn't believe this tiny Oriental slut could take both of us for such a long time." (Remember, its title was *Asian Fuck Toys.*)

On the worksheet which all of the tribunal members kept in preparation for each hearing I wrote in the space beside the title *Asian Fuck Toys* "U.I. [Unconditionally Indecent] See caption about 'tiny Oriental slut.' Model looks underage. Rape. Title—'fuck toys.'" This was the type of material that we saw as demeaning or treating "as inherently inferior or unequal any person or group of persons, which are not serious treatments" by means of "the close-up depiction of genitalia or other body parts, and other depictions which reduce a person to her or his sexual parts."

You will note that I have directly quoted here material that I considered to be unconditionally indecent. The material is unconditionally indecent when it appears in a glossy magazine that is designed, as one commentator expressed it, as a "male masturbatory aid" (Scott, 1991). The same words, however, are "not indecent" when removed from this context (the magazine with its "arousing" photographs) and placed in the context of an academic analysis. This illustrates the point that it is not what is depicted but the manner of depiction that makes the difference between indecent and permissible publications. One can depict a rape if it is a "serious treatment."

In deciding whether a publication violated the second guideline, we were sometimes reduced to considering the camera angle. It was possible, for example, to photograph a lesbian couple making love with the help of a dildo in a way which expressed mutuality and pleasure. Photographed differently, however, the same series of activities may reduce the women to "holes waiting to be poked." The line was extremely hard to draw and we agonized and argued over whether to ban some of these explicit magazines which, either way, were nothing more than sexist trash. The deciding issue was usually violence.

In the course of 6 years, I read about 10,000 pornographic publications. The more violent material came disproportionately from the United States. Nadine Strossen (1995) has commented that

[American] society's wariness toward sex is highlighted by contrasting it with the greater societal tolerance toward violence. This dichotomy is especially vivid in the media and mass culture, where violent depictions are far more accepted than sexual ones. The contrast was aptly capsulized by Martin Shafer, a top executive at a film company, when he noted, "If a man touches a woman's breast in a movie, it's an R rating, but if he cuts off a limb with a chain saw, it's a PG–13." (p. 21)

The cultural difference in the levels of tolerance of violence between the United States and countries like Britain, New Zealand, and Australia was illustrated by our differential levels of acceptance of certain magazines that we judged as clearly and consistently violating the second guideline. We banned the American magazine *Hustler*, which is so mainstream in some American states that I have seen it displayed unsealed alongside *Playboy* and similar "soft" magazines about which we had few if any concerns. I recall banning one U.S. magazine because it contained a "joke" cartoon depicting an ax-murderers' convention. Laughing men were surrounding a cake on the top of which was a model of the dismembered body of a woman. Rape, racism, and other forms of sexual violence are placed by some U.S. magazines in a context of male masturbatory eroticism. These are not legally available in New Zealand. North American radical feminist definitions of pornography (such as the McKinnon-Dworkin definition) are premised upon the availability of this kind of material. They define pornography *as* this sort of material.

SOME ACADEMIC QUESTIONS

By 1992 there had been further changes in the membership of the tribunal. Keri Hulme had completed her term of office and was replaced by a new expert in literature, Anne Holden, author of crime novels. She was over 60 years of age and therefore added a valuable older generational experience to the collective knowledge of the tribunal. The criminologist had also left and was replaced by a member of the Maori Arts Council. The two lawyers who had participated in the *Penthouse Decision* (including the chair, Peter Cartwright) continued to serve. I now found myself the longest serving member of the tribunal. I shall briefly list some of the more interesting and difficult final decisions that raised questions about freedom of expression and which were sometimes the basis of disagreement and debate between the tribunal members as we sought to formulate coherent policies.

In our *Penthouse Decision* (described above), we had grappled with the implications for our work of the recently passed Bill of Rights Act, of

1990.[11] This stated that "everyone has the right to freedom of expression, including the freedom to seek, receive, and impart information and opinions of any kind in any form" (S 14). Could censorship be compatible with this guarantee of freedom of expression? The act stated that "the rights and freedoms contained in this Bill of Rights may be subject only to such reasonable limits prescribed by law as can be demonstrably justified in a free and democratic society" (S 5). Where there was doubt about the permissibility of a publication, the Bill of Rights required us to come down on the side of freedom of expression: "Whenever an enactment can be given a meaning that is consistent with the rights and freedoms contained in this Bill of Rights, that meaning shall be preferred to any other meaning" (S 6).

From 1990, the rights and freedoms of those who enjoyed unusual sexual practices were considered. In a special hearing to consider fetish magazines involving consensual sexual violence, such as bondage and discipline, we heard evidence (directly and via counsel) from, among others, gay and heterosexual sadomasochists, sex workers from bondage and discipline parlors, and psychotherapists.[12] A feminist analysis of unequal power relations between men and women was supported by evidence from, among others, therapists who work with convicted sex offenders. As a result, eroticized images of bound women were more likely to be banned by us than were images of men who were bound in a play-acting situation by a dominatrix. Within British magazines of this genre, a recurrent theme was that of being caned in a school setting. There were many depictions of adult men dressed as schoolboys and being caned by nubile, seminaked female teachers. Not all of the publications submitted to us concerned sex, for, as stated in the Indecent Publications Act, our terms of reference were also to classify publications concerning matters of "horror, crime, cruelty or violence in a manner that is injurious to the public good." I developed a modified libertarian position that the public good could best be served by censorship decisions that both protected the vulnerable from exploitation and that sought, simultaneously, to maintain the "free and democratic society" envisaged in documents like New Zealand's Bill of Rights Act and the U.S. First Amendment. Some of the distinguishing features of such a society are freedom of speech, the freedom to dissent from majority opinion, and the freedom to work peacefully for changes in the laws that govern and regulate our daily lives.

Some of our most contentious debates concerned "drugs and bombs" (Middleton, 1994). In a free and democratic society, one should, for example, be free to advocate changes in the law with respect to the cultivation, distribution, and consumption of marijuana. Simple how-to-grow-marijuana manuals were traditionally banned by the tribunal (they advocate, and instruct in, the commission of crime), whereas marijuana smokers lifestyle magazines, which may have value to those working for law reform, sometimes received an age restriction.

There were also heated discussions among tribunal members over American survivalist publications, including manuals on how to manufacture explosives from agricultural and other common ingredients and how to conduct terrorist operations using these. While some tribunal members saw these as providing purely technical information, I took a more conservative line on at least one occasion and recommended banning. The lawyers on the tribunal described the making of explosives as "not illegal," the growing of marijuana as illegal, and thus the bomb manuals as less bannable than the dope growers guides. As a nonlawyer, I saw the issue differently. Everyone knew that the growing of marijuana was illegal, and if one chose to break this law, the greatest danger was getting arrested for it. If one chose to make a bomb one could kill an innocent party. The public good was more likely to be injured by the latter than the former.

Occasionally, sound recordings were referred to the tribunal. For example, in 1992 the New Zealand Police Association was granted leave by the minister of justice to refer the recording *Body Count* by the U.S. rap musician Ice T and the band Public Enemy. Along with their American and Australian counterparts, New Zealand Police were particularly concerned about the song "Cop Killer." In giving the album the classification of "not indecent," the tribunal argued that "to sing about violence is not to commit violence. The song is not exhortory. It expresses the genuine frustration of many young American blacks with the Los Angeles police force, and indeed the lyrics of 'Cop Killer' . . . put the song clearly in that context" (Decision 100/92). This, like other tribunal decisions with respect to "matters of sex, horror, crime, cruelty or violence" rested on a concept of the public good that was grounded in the assumption of a pluralistic democracy that tolerated a broad range of personal moralities within a common legal framework protecting the rights and freedoms of minorities.

THE NEW ORDER

By 1992 new censorship legislation was long overdue. It made sense to bring under one umbrella the previously separate classification processes and criteria for films, videos, and printed publications. There were anachronisms in the old acts (Middleton, 1994). And in the case of our tribunal—a group of five citizens who were employed part-time to represent "the community"—it was becoming increasingly difficult to cope with the ever-increasing quantity of sexually explicit publications.

Many years of lobbying by community groups preceded and influenced the ways in which the new legislation was conceptualized. The fourth Labour Government (1984–1990) had experienced strong lobbying from anti-pornography feminists within the Labour Party. It had set up a commission of inquiry (Morris et al., 1989) and drafted a new bill before the 1990 election. During the election campaign, the opposition National Party also made the proposed new legislation an election issue. Candidates announced in the media that National would "ban child pornography" and "violent pornography," but few, if any, of their public statements mentioned the fact that such materials were already illegal. Since only the most extreme libertarians would not support the banning of these things, and since there was very little public awareness of existing censorship criteria and policies, the spirit of the new legislation was generally received as a good thing. Shortly after its election victory, the National government redrafted Labour's proposed bill, set up a select committee—to which the Indecent Publications Tribunal made a submission (1992)—and passed the Films, Videos and Publications Classification Act late in 1992.

There was little public discussion or criticism of this act. Perhaps few were prepared to run the risk of being accused of defending pornography or sexism. Even the civil liberties groups were curiously silent. Visiting American feminist philosopher Alison Jaggar (1993) wondered if the act were "so broadly drawn that it could be used to prohibit expression of all kinds of ideas." Similarly, a writer surmised that "the likely effect of this new statute is a censorship regime that is excessively repressive" (p. 84). At the time of writing (January 1997), the climate with respect to censorship remains liberal. However, the new legislation has, I believe, created the possibilities for the repression of information and ideas if a more conservative series of appointments to the censorship apparatus were made. There are some potentially serious implications for research, and for education.

The Films, Videos and Publications Classification Act created two tiers of bannable material. The second tier allowed for the censors' discretion (Middleton, 1994). It is the first tier which could cause problems for artists, writers, and researchers. The new act replaced the term *indecent* with the word *objectionable*. Objectionable is defined as follows:

> 3. meaning of "objectionable"—(1) For the purposes of this Act, a publication is objectionable if it describes, depicts, expresses, or otherwise deals with matters such as sex, horror, crime, cruelty, or violence in such a manner that the availability of the publication is likely to be injurious to the public good.
>
>   (2) A publication shall be deemed to be objectionable for the purposes of this Act if the publication promotes or supports, or tends to promote or support,-

(a) The exploitation of children or young persons, or both, for sexual purposes; or
(b) The use of violence or coercion to compel any person to participate in, or submit to, sexual conduct; or
(c) Sexual conduct with or upon the body of a dead person; or
(d) the use of urine or excrement in association with degrading or dehumanising conduct or sexual conduct; or
(e) Bestiality; or
(f) Acts of torture or the infliction of extreme violence or extreme cruelty

An objectionable publication has to be banned—by order of Parliament—and, with respect to publications in this category, the statute does not seem to allow for a censor's discretion. Possession of such objectionable materials becomes a criminal offense.

To illustrate some educational questions about this, let me take as an example one of the first feminist doctoral theses to be completed in New Zealand (Seymour, 1981). Central to this sociological study was a feminist analysis of the persecution of witches. A key resource was the *Malleus Maleficarum* (the handbook of the Spanish Inquisition)—a document which undoubtedly "promotes or supports . . . acts of torture or the infliction of extreme violence or extreme cruelty." Similarly, Hitler's *Mein Kampf*—a reading which is essential for many historians—advocates the extermination of Jews and other "races" deemed to be inferior to Aryans. Some myths can be read, and are often visually depicted, as supporting or promoting bestiality. As it is written, those whose job it is to implement the act could find themselves in the unfortunate situation of having to prohibit, or severely limit access to, historical texts which are needed for research. Works of art and literature, such as the novels of the Marquis de Sade (classified as not indecent by the Indecent Publications Tribunal) could once again be in danger of prohibition as they were in the 1920s (Dugdale, 1994; Perry, 1965, 1980).

This circumscribing of objectionable materials could have the effect of limiting the freedom of expression of political opinion. For example, on one occasion, the tribunal allowed to pass a Californian newsletter from a law reform organization that, in early-1960s sexual-revolution style, wanted to legalize sex between adults and "consenting children." The newsletter included a code of ethics that contained strong statements against breaking the law and stated the group's policy of refusing to publish or forward any pedophilic erotica or use the newsletter as a forum or point of contact between subscribers. The newsletter itself contained excerpts from the works of noted sexologists and others concerning child sexuality and the law. It provided space for the articulation of ideas which are repulsive to probably the vast majority of the population. New Zealand's new legislation can be seen as endangering the right to freedom of expression of opinion because it lists topics which one is no longer allowed to write about or express in visual media. In 1963 the Indecent Publications Act defined indecency in terms of the manner of depiction, but the 1993 legislation's first-tier category creates the space for prohibiting representations of certain topics and allows the manner of depiction to be taken into account only with respect to the second tier (Middleton, 1994). Thus it can be seen as raising the kinds of issues that are presently being raised by the screening out of key words (topics) on the Internet.

It is necessary to have legislation that will screen out child pornography and material which eroticizes rape and other nonconsensual acts of violence. However, in a free and democratic society, it is also essential to preserve the accessibility of historic texts, to protect the rights of sexual and other minorities to freedom of expression, and to allow for the articulation of deviant opinions such as the writings of law reform groups and the publication of radical political tracts.

I have gone into some detail to tell you about the lived complexities involved in determining the meaning of the word *indecent*. Such processes were a result of public and government demands for the surveillance, monitoring, and regulation of erotic and violent printed matter, then films, and more recently, videos. The Internet is much more complex. One cannot go to all this expense and trouble over every sexual message or image. Recently there have been cases of New Zealand teenagers downloading some of the survivalist books the tribunal had banned and making the bombs from the instructions found in them. These publications also included instructions on how to kill people and get away with it. The blocking of the alt.sex news groups by my university can be seen by those who seek access to it as only a minor nuisance, since one can (though at greater expense) dial a file server elsewhere and access alt.sex through that. The disciplinary apparatuses of censorship that were developed for the age of print cannot work in the electronic age.

DISCIPLINING THE VIRTUAL BODY

Mark Poster (1990, 1995) has coined the term *mode of information*. He suggests that

> history may be periodized by variations in the structure . . . of symbolic exchange. . . . Stages in the mode of information may be tentatively designated as follows: face-to-face socially mediated exchange; written ex

changes mediated by print; and electronically mediated exchange. . . . In
the first, oral stage the self is constituted as a position of enunciation
through its embeddedness in a totality of face-to-face relations. In the
second, print stage the self is constructed as an agent, centered in ra-
tional/imaginary autonomy. In the third, electronic stage the self is de-
centered, dispersed, and multiplied in continuous instability. (p. 6)

Drawing on Foucault, Poster points out that these three modes of information should not be viewed as a teleology and that today they exist simultaneously. For example, researching for this book has involved me in all three.
The "face-to-face socially mediated exchanges" have included conducting
life-history interviews with teachers, participating in tribunal hearings, and
being interviewed in connection with a grant application. The "written
exchanges mediated by print" were writing to and reading letters from my
interviewees; writing applications for grants; organizing the transcribing
of tapes into print, and reading and writing tribunal decisions. And the
"electronically mediated exchanges" included compiling a NUD-IST computer database, interacting with my publishers and colleagues via e-mail,
and surfing the Internet for information about U.S. censorship law.

Speaking of the post–World War II baby boom, Dale Spender (1995)
argues that

we are the last generation to be reared within a culture in which print is
the primary information medium. Because we have grown up and become
skilled in a print-based community, we have developed certain ways of
making sense of the world. We are, to some extent, what print has made
us. And now we have to change. (p. xv)

There is, she argues, "a new flexibility associated with the electronic media
which is at odds with the very idea of standardization and regulation" (p.
14). Print has characterized the modern (or industrial) age—the age of
standardization in which emerged the various bodies of knowledge (academic disciplines) to which as teachers and members of professional organizations, we bear allegiance (Harvey, 1990; Lyotard, 1984). It has also been
formative of the regulatory apparatuses with which such knowledge and
information have been policed—censorship, copyright, and the mechanisms
through which academic standards are established and monitored. What
are the implications of this postmodern age for the disciplining of sexuality/
the body?

This discussion of censorship—the regulation of words and pictures—
has moved me away from Foucault's object of analysis, the disciplining of
the corporeal body. Does Foucault's work have value in helping us to think

about the disciplining of virtual bodies—images and information—in the electronic age?

Foucault's work has been used in several discussions of power-knowledge and electronic databases (Lyotard, 1984; Poster, 1990, 1995). Foucault saw power in modern (industrial) societies as panoptic, an architectural metaphor that he drew from Jeremy Bentham's (1791) design for a prison. Panoptic surveillance required bodies to be congregated in architectural spaces designated for particular forms of disciplinary surveillance— schools, prisons, asylums, hospitals, and so on (Foucault, 1977). Within these disciplinary apparatuses, people know that they are being watched for some of the time—by teachers, guards, psychiatrists, doctors, and so forth—and that information is being gathered and stored about them. Knowing that we are being watched for some of the time encourages conformity all of the time. This metaphor of the all-seeing eye of power in architectural spaces has been extended into conceptualizations of the gathering, storage, and distribution of information about individuals in the various apparatuses of electronic surveillance (Lyotard, 1984; Poster, 1990):

> Today's "circuits of communication" and the databases they generate constitute a superpanopticon, a system of surveillance without walls, windows, towers or guards. . . . the populace has been disciplined to surveillance and to participating in the process. Social security cards, drivers' licenses, credit cards and the like—the individual must apply for them, have them ready at all times, use them continually. (Poster, 1990, p. 93)

This has implications for sexuality and the body. An example is the way the sex lives of single mothers are policed. Those applying for or receiving welfare benefits are forbidden to have regular sex with a man in a relationship which could be construed as similar to a marriage. There have been cases of neighbors reporting single mothers' sexual activities to welfare authorities.

Foucault died in 1984. He was a product of his time and did not experience the full impact of the Internet (Macey, 1995). To think about the electronic media we will need additional theorists.

DISCUSSION

The Internet has major implications for disciplining sexuality, and the conceptualizations and mechanisms of censorship that were designed in the industrial, modern age of print will not work in a postmodern electronic environment. As discussed in this chapter, parents worry about their children gaining access to pornography on the World Wide Web. Technologies to assist parental surveillance are already on the market in the form of special software for computers and "v chips" for satellite television. E-mail news groups have been of concern to some women, who have warned that the Internet is crowded with male sexual predators waiting to pounce at each click of a female user's mouse (Spender, 1995). Other feminists have embraced the opportunities that e-mail offers for interactive forms of writing (Cherny & Weise, 1996; Middleton, 1996b). There are accounts of "love on the Net," of "virtual sex," and of Internet users who create fictitious personae that float in cyberspace — men who write as women, women who write as men (Cherny & Weise, 1996).

In cyberspace we are freed from the face-to-face socially mediated politics of embodiment — attractiveness of appearance, the markings of skin color, the visible signs of poverty (dress or nutrition), or gender. We are freed from the "rational" print-induced hierarchies of academic, professional, or financial status or rank. What are "out there" (nowhere/everywhere) are not bodies, but simulacra — copies without originals (Lather, 1990; Poster, 1990). As Mark Poster (1990) has argued,

> Words cannot any longer be located in space and time, whether it be the "real time" of spoken utterance in a spatial context of presence or the abstract time of documents in a bureaucrat's file cabinet or library's archive. Speech is framed by space/time coordinates of dramatic action. Writing is framed by space/time coordinates of books and sheets of paper. Both are available to logics of representation. Electronic language, on the contrary, does not lend itself to being so framed. It is everywhere and nowhere, always and never. It is truly material/immaterial. (p. 85)

Who will gain access to the unimaginable riches of cyberspace? Can equality of access and opportunity be guaranteed (Lyotard, 1984)? What knowledge and information will be available, by whom, and to whom? What power relations will govern life on the Net? Are schools an anachronism of the industrial, modern age of print? Will the principal location of researching, learning, and teaching be cyberspace? These are some of the issues we face as we move into the new millennium.

CHAPTER FIVE

Embodying Educational Theory

Underpinning this book has been a pedagogical strategy. The education and sexuality course for which it is to be a resource is part of several programs, including the education studies, or theory, strand of a preservice teaching degree. In many parts of the Western world today, theory as a component of such teacher education programs is described as being under threat (Apple, 1996a, 1996b; Verma, 1992). Sandra Acker (1995) has argued that in Britain,

> spurred by a series of highly-publicised right-wing critiques that assigned to teacher education the blame for subversive and dogmatically progressive education, government control of the curriculum of higher education seriously weakened the old tradition of foundation disciplines, so that "theory" is disappearing in the wake of a consuming emphasis on learning through practical experience. (p. 60)

Similarly, writing from Australia, Erica McWilliam (1995) comments that

> in six years I have seen the demise of the foundational disciplines as educational "theory." Psychology, sociology, and philosophy have been doled out in increasingly small measure because more pedagogical territory was demanded for curriculum "basics" and fieldwork. (p. 4)

However, too often the disciplines and fields of educational theory (sociology, philosophy, psychology, history, policy studies, etc.) have appeared in classes in the form of decontextualized and disembodied abstractions—as charts drawn by those with the expertise to depict "what is there" on the educational terrain. International debates in educational theory, and historical processes of policy formation, appeared to some students as "abstracted from particular participants located in particular spatio-temporal settings" (D. Smith, 1987, p. 61). In teaching educational theory as somehow external to students—as the intellectual property of remote (and, for New Zealanders, usually overseas) academics—we alienate students from their own educational perspectives.

Preservice, practicing, and former teachers' perceptions of the irrelevance of, or pessimism in, some educational theory and policy courses have been documented in recent research (Clandinin & Connelly, 1995; McWilliam, 1995; Middleton, 1996d; Middleton & May, 1997). Can we teach theory and policy as the intellectual productions of "real people," solving educational problems in the everyday world? Can we heal the (Descartian) mind–body split—the gulf between theory and practice—by putting the body back into theory? As Clandinin & Connelly (1995) have argued,

> Teachers' lives take shape because of their professional knowledge landscapes. They draw on their individual biographies, on the particular histories of the professional landscape in which they find themselves, on how they are positioned on the landscape, and on the form of everyday school life that the professional landscape allows. (p. 27)

Rather than position students as readers of others' theoretical maps, can we address them as on the terrain—as inside the phenomena they are studying? And can we thereby shift students' and policymakers' perceptions of theory so that "embodied theory" is seen as central to a practical teacher education?

To help me methodologically (in the allied enterprises of research and teaching), I have drawn heavily on Foucault's work as a "tool kit" (Foucault, 1980b, p. 143). There is, writes Gyatri Spivak (1990), a certain irony on the part of "enthusiastic academic intellectuals who, at the same time, swallow Foucault's critique of the watershed intellectual and make Foucault into a watershed intellectual" (p. 56). With respect to this, Foucault's biographer, David Macey (1995), tells the following cautionary tale:

> Jana Sawicki [1991] had just spent four years writing a doctoral dissertation on Foucault's critique of humanism and attempting to "appropriate" it for feminism. The day after she submitted it for examination, she had the opportunity to attend part of Foucault's Vermont seminar. "I told him that I had just finished writing a dissertation on his critique of humanism. Not surprisingly he responded with some embarrassment and much seriousness. He suggested that I do not spend energy talking about him and, instead, do what he was doing, namely, write genealogies." (p. 450)

Rather than treat Foucault as a theorist in the sense of a master of truth and justice, I have used his method of genealogy to support my own minute investigations into how "the West has managed . . . to annex sex to a field of rationality" (Dreyfus & Rabinow, 1982, p. 79). I have adopted his suspicions of "descending" theoretical frameworks, and his suggestion that instead we "conduct ascending analysis of power, starting, that is, from its infinitesimal mechanisms" (Foucault, 1980b, p. 98). "It is," he said, "not theory, but life that matters, not knowledge, but reality" (1980b, p. 81). The "role for theory today," he argued, is "not to formulate the global systematic theory which holds everything in place, but to analyse the specificity of mechanisms of power, to locate the connections and extensions, to build little by little a strategic knowledge" (p. 145).

This use of Foucault may appear problematic to those critical policy scholars who take a stronger neo-Marxist position than I do and also to those who place themselves more fully within a liberal-progressive discourse—for both of these see history as evolutionary, or teleological. As Paul Patton (1979) explains, Foucault expressed "opposition to all philosophies of history. For genealogy, there is no Reason or Ruse at work in history. That capitalist production or the carceral should have arisen when and where it did is a purely contingent matter" (p. 140). For Foucault, Patton points out, "history is a process without a subject, or rather, it may be described from the standpoint of any number of subjects, and for Foucault, for the moment, the 'subject' is power itself" (p. 124). How then, ask Dreyfus and Rabinow (1982), can we

> talk about intentionality without a subject, a strategy without a strategist? The answer must lie in the practices themselves. For it is the practices, focused in technologies and innumerable, separate localizations, which literally embody what the analyst is seeking to understand. (p. 187)

Within this perspective, Marxism, liberalism, and the whole of Western science, appear as *historically constructed* discourses, that are multiply and variously located in relation to the "ruling apparatus" (D. Smith, 1987). It is this which makes Foucault a postmodernist writer and for which he has been accused of relativism and nihilism (Paglia, 1995). However, there is one universal in Foucault's thought—that history is "inscribed" on the body. As David Harvey (1990) explains, Foucault

> treats the space of the body as the irreducible element in our social scheme of things, for it is upon that space that the forces of repression, socialization, disciplining, and punishing are inflicted. The body exists in space and must either submit to authority (through, for example, incarceration or surveillance in an organized space) or carve out particular spaces of resistance and freedom—"heterotopias"—from an otherwise repressive world. (p. 213)

A healthy skepticism about the possibilities of totalizing narratives or "truths" does not mean that researchers and professionals should cease to make use of the academic disciplines to think about the world, do our research, and engage in political activism. In the past two decades, many feminist and postcolonial writers have used Foucault's work in combination with various Marxisms and other theories, such as psychoanalysis or liberal notions of democracy and equality. Such blendings as "materialist feminism" (Barrett, 1991; Hennessey, 1993; Middleton, 1993a, 1993b; Weiner, 1994) and "postcolonialism" (Bhabha, 1994; Said, 1993; Spivak, 1990) have proved useful tool kits with which to uncover how the power-knowledges of political philosophy, natural and social science, professional practices, and curriculum subjects bear the cultural inscriptions of their time and place—such as those of imperialism, class, and gender. Edward Said (1993) has outlined such a standpoint for social research:

> The map of the world has no divinely or dogmatically sanctioned spaces, essences, or privileges. However, we may speak of secular spaces, and of humanly constructed and interdependent histories that are fundamentally knowable, although not through grand theory or systematic totalisation. . . . human experience is finely textured, dense, and accessible enough *not* to need extra-historical or extra-worldly agencies to illuminate or explain it. I am talking about a way of regarding our world as amenable to investigation without magic keys, special jargons and instruments. (p. 377)

Rather than lapsing into the relativistic chaos of which postmodernist scholars are often accused (Paglia, 1995), postcolonial and feminist scholars who write as consciously situated intellectuals are writing "a new history which is more aware of its status as narrative and which is at least suspicious of, if not rejecting outright, the universal and disengaged subject of empiricism" (Hennessey, 1993, p. 101).

No longer conceptualizing ourselves as disengaged observers, many postmodernist researchers have included in our written accounts the situated story of our researching and writing processes and interactions—"investigations into the conditions of possibility which make certain meanings allowable and which also acknowledge their own historicity" (Hennessey, 1993, p. 7). The "historicity" or experiential grounding of our own accounts is seen as a legitimate part of our research problem and topic of inclusion as we seek to study in our own works "the determinative powers of discourse in constituting practices that are intimately responsible for what Said has described as "how people thought, lived and spoke" (Barrett, 1991, p. 131)—including our own research inquiries and teaching practice.

The inclusion of the standpoint from which the authorial voice originates in the writing of research, and the teaching of courses, is not a license for undisciplined self-indulgence. Rather, if done well, it can help us to do "better science" by making visible to the reader the processes which are hidden beneath the mask of disembodied uninvolvement that traditional accounts have required. What are the historical, political, and cultural circumstances in which certain types of research questions get asked? Which of them are made possible and why (through access to supervision, funding, etc.)? How and why were particular methodological choices made (such as whether to do ethnography or life-history)? What were the conditions of possibility for the choice of analytic and interpretive techniques, such as symbolic interactionism, grounded theory, or deconstruction? How and why have particular concepts or theories been used (neo-Marxism, behaviorism, feminism, etc.)? Postmodernist writings problematize these issues as a central part of the research.

The wider educational research community, however, has tended to marginalize such positions. Although there is a strong feminist presence at conferences such as the American Educational Research Association (AERA), many of the sessions at which feminist theoretical contributions are debated in detail and depth seldom attract the attention of male critical theorists. The following statement comes from Gillian Rose (1993), who is a geographer, but what she is saying about her discipline applies just as well to education as a field of academic study. She describes the relationships between feminists and "others" in her field

> not as a series of conversations between equals, but more as a series of brush-offs. Feminism has been consistently marginalized by mainstream geography. . . . Papers may contain a one off [an isolated] reference or two to feminist authors, and a feminist chapter or two, written by some combination of the valiant few feminist geographers, is obligatory now in most edited collections, but there is hardly ever a sustained engagement with feminist work. (p. 3)

As Carmen Luke (1992) puts it, "To cite 'key' feminist authors in the burial site of the bibliography is not the same as knowing or using their work" (p. 40).

The feminist research that fits into the dominant conceptual and methodological traditions of scholarship in education studies (quantitative analyses, ethnographies, etc.) is more likely to have been woven into its mainstream teaching texts. However, it has been largely, but not exclusively, feminists who have experimented with narrative modes of inquiry and forms of writing—especially reflexive improvisations that interweave personal (autobiographical), theoretical, and contextual (political, historical, etc.) dimensions (Hughes, Lovell, Preston & Martin, 1995). The continuing marginalizations of feminist theoretical work, then, has also resulted in the marginalization of the narrative methodologies and writing styles that feminists have disproportionately favored. There is, as I have argued here, a large body of (mostly, but not exclusively, feminist) writing that exemplifies the growing tradition of research that includes a strand of situated autobiography (Biklen, 1995; Luke & Gore, 1992a; Middleton, 1993a, 1993b; Jones, 1991; Silin, 1995; Spivak, 1990). There is also a foundational literature that articulates strong rationales — theoretical, pedagogical, professional, and methodological — for doing so (Jones, 1992; Smith, 1987, 1990). Whereas some of the reflexive studies are occasionally cited in mainstream texts, the feminist theoretical debates upon which these studies are grounded are seldom engaged with in depth by "other" critical theorists.

In several edited collections (Apple, 1995–1996; Witherel and Noddings, 1991), examples of feminist and "other" reflexive narrative studies have been brought together. In the introduction to his most recent book, *Cultural Politics and Education*, Michael Apple (1996a) outlines the concerns some leftist writers have expressed about reflexive work: "such writing can serve the chilling function of simply saying, 'But enough about you, let me tell you about me', unless we are much more reflexive about this that has often been the case" (p. xiv). Such critics, he says, worry that the inclusion of the authorial voice in research accounts can "wind up privileging the white, middle-class woman's or man's need for self-display" (p. xiv). They ask:

> Is the insistence on the personal, an insistence that underpins much of our turn to literary and autobiographical form, partly a class discourse as well? The "personal may be political," but does the political end at the personal? Furthermore, why should we assume that the personal is any less difficult to understand than the "external" world? (p. xiv)

In contrast to such "bourgeois" personal narratives, Apple formulates his own "personal story" as "*consciously* connected to a clear sense of the realities of structurally generated inequalities that play such a large part in education" (p. xiv). Although Apple has elsewhere demonstrated a familiarity with feminist materialist and other consciously reflexive writings (Apple, 1995–1996), in this latter text he does not acknowledge this body of theoretical work. In this text he renders invisible the bedrock, or precedent, upon which his own case for situated theorizing could have been made.

The equation of the "I" with bourgeois individualism alone is foreign to me, since I come from New Zealand, where the indigenous Maori have an oral tradition that requires us to state our whakapapa [genealogy] — to say who we are—before speaking about politics, theory, or other subjects (Pere, 1988). To be bourgeois in the social sciences or education is NOT to speak personally—it is to hide one's perspectivity behind a mask of disembodied objectivity.

In this book, I have taken the theme of disciplining sexuality and traced it contrapuntally as it surfaced in policy texts, archival materials, interview data, and my own experience. This contrapuntal reading—from the top, the bottom, and the spaces in between, serves to "underline the fact that the state's power (and that's one of the reasons for its strength) is both a totalizing and an individualizing kind of power" (Foucault, 1982, p. 213). When one's research focus is the body, the class and political dynamics of the global economy are continually manifested through stories about Pacific Islands children copying the clothing, language, and demeanor of Black rappers in American music videos; in the "mis-match" between American pornography and New Zealanders' tolerance for it; through the marketing of packaged programs in our schools. Foucault's approach can, as Keith Hoskin (1990) and others have pointed out (Henriques et al., 1984), help collapse old binaries and provide "a new construct for comprehending the stubbornly different levels of explanation usually known as the 'sociological' and the 'psychological', and with a clue to the secret . . . of its operation" (p. 52). And this is the focus from which we need to teach "situated theory" in teacher education courses. In our writing and teaching, we can use such a standpoint to raise questions about the circumstances in which we ask research questions, engage in research encounters with others, analyze and interpret these, and write about them.

As I finish this book, I think of the power relations behind its production. It too is in history—has been brought into being and shaped within international academic and commercial relations. The language I use and the material I select have been shaped by the audience that is its "market." The opportunity to write results from economic, academic, and institutional circumstances both locally and globally. As Foucault (1977) says,

> We should admit . . . that power produces knowledge (and not simply by encouraging it because it serves power or by applying it because it is useful); that power and knowledge directly imply one another; that there is no power relation without the correlative constitution of a field of knowledge, nor any knowledge that does not predispose and constitute at the same time power relations. (p. 27)

As another academic year starts, I am preparing to learn how to teach via the Internet—using both e-mail and the World Wide Web. Our work is being transformed in a postmodern age of electronics. Increasingly we who teach and do research experience ourselves and our intellectual communities as nodes in multiple and intersecting networks rather than as individuals in hierarchies; authorship as ephemeral and communal; theories as fragmented and concepts as floating between disciplines; data as auditory or visual, static or moving; writing as the construction of collages, pastiches and juxtapositions rather than linear text. And, by the form in which I have chosen to present this book, I hope to have demonstrated some of these practices—which have also been part of its object of study. These are some of the new circumstances in which new questions will be addressed in our teaching and research as we—our corporeal and our virtual bodies—move into the new millennium.

Notes

INTRODUCTION

1. NUD-IST is the acronym for Non-numerical Unstructured Data Indexing, Searching and Theorizing — a program developed by QSR Corp Pty, La Trobe University, Box 171, Victoria 3083, Australia. The stories I tell in Chapters One and Two were collected during 1994 and 1995, when I did 75 life-history interviews for an oral history of educational ideas as lived by New Zealand teachers from 1915–1995. Between us, Helen May and I asked 150 men and women teachers and former teachers — the oldest born in 1899 and the youngest in 1973 — to talk about how they had come to develop their personal philosophies of education. We asked them to talk about formative influences in their upbringing, their schooling, their decisions to go into teaching, their training, and their teaching careers. While Helen interviewed early childhood and infant teachers, my interviews were of those who taught high school, junior high, and older elementary school students. Helen and I each created our own separate NUD-IST databases from the 75 interviews we each conducted. Our collaborative results were published in Middleton & May, 1997. I created a "minidatabase" especially for this present book. It drew only on my own interviews, and was indexed in a separate NUD-IST *tree* (or category) from the two main databases that we each constructed for our collaborative oral history project (Middleton & May, 1997). The database used in Chapters One and Two of the present book consists of all the material from my 75 interviews pertaining to discipline and sexuality. These two chapters are revisions of a conference paper (Middleton, 1996a) which I had completed before beginning to write the collaborative text with Helen May. More details of the methodology of our collaborative wider study are in Middleton, 1996b.

2. For details about Chapters One and Two, see note 1. The life-history interview data in Chapter Three come from a previously unpublished chapter of my doctoral thesis (Middleton, 1985). Further details of the thesis from which the data in this chapter were extracted are in Middleton, 1987/1994 and Middleton, 1993a. The source of material in Chapter Four is my 6 years' working in censorship on New Zealand's Indecent Publications Tribunal. This is explained in full in the chapter itself and also in Middleton, 1994.

3. The term *Western* is problematic for those of us who reside in the southern hemisphere, since it presumes a northern perspective on the globe.

CHAPTER ONE

1. The original collaborative project for which these data were gathered included early childhood institutions and primary and secondary schools. Because of our differing teaching backgrounds and research interests, Helen May collected and analyzed data on early childhood and infant teaching, whereas my focus was on the experiences and teaching of pupils in the senior classes in primary schools, in intermediate (junior high) schools, and in secondary schools (Middleton & May, 1997). The data in this present text concentrates on my secondary school material.

2. I have chosen to use an archaeological metaphor here because it is particularly appropriate. In his early books Foucault himself described his method as "archaeology" and was concerned primarily with the historical emergence of discourses as coherent conceptual systems of thought. Later, however, he made connections between discourses and power and formulated his notion of "power-knowledge." He then described his method as "genealogy." However, most writers see this as a shift in emphasis rather than as a break (Dreyfus & Rabinow, 1982; Gordon, 1980; Macey, 1995; Patton, 1979; Sheridan, 1980). My own work draws on Foucault's writings after his shift to genealogy (Foucault, 1977, 1980a, 1980b, 1982). However, as the above writers argue, he never abandoned the idea of archaeology entirely.

3. The Enlightenment refers to the post–French Revolution emphasis on reason as the supreme human virtue and as the basis for the government of democracies. As the legitimating ideology of industrial capitalism, liberalism (the philosophy of individual freedom and autonomy) argued that positions of power and authority must be a reward of merit—individual talent and hard work. During this period (since the eighteenth century) the industrial revolution and the urbanization of populations stimulated the growth of the regulatory apparatuses studied by Foucault.

CHAPTER TWO

1. The term *sex* is commonly used to refer to the biological dimension and *gender* to the cultural/social. This binary distinction, however, has been severely challenged by feminist scientists. They have deconstructed biology as a science to show that it mirrors cultural (including sexist) mores. Furthermore, they have argued that the body itself is in part a cultural construction (Gilbert, 1996; Harding, 1987; Tuana, 1989). This book is concerned with the body. However, feminist histories of gender (concerning women's social roles and beliefs about them) also contain useful material on historical conceptualizations of the body.

2. *Native schools* (later termed *Maori schools*) differed from the regular public primary schools in that they were administered by the Department of Native Affairs (later Maori Affairs) rather than by the regional education boards. Their curricula were similar to the board schools, although by the 1930s innovative administrators began to emphasise Maori culture as part of the curriculum (Barrington & Beaglehole, 1974; Openshaw, Lee, & Lee, 1993). Pakeha children who lived in the predominantly Maori areas where there were Native schools usually attended the Na-

tive school and Maori children in towns attended the regular board schools. This system was phased out by 1968 once Maori became a more urban population. Since the mid-1980s, a renewed enthusiasm for schools which emphasize Maori language and culture has fuelled the establishment of separate preschools and schools (Irwin, 1990; Smith, 1990).

3. My data suggest that in many educational settings returned servicemen became a force for change. As teachers in training, they were more likely than their school-leaver peers to question the practices of their lecturers and as teachers to challenge the ideas of their senior colleagues (Middleton, 1996c; Middleton & May, 1997).

4. See note 5.

5. According to Rangimarie Rose Pere (1988), Maori traditions in her tribe encouraged openness in discussions about sexuality. However, the colonial influence, especially among urban families, no doubt introduced British notions of reticence on sexual matters to Maori child-rearing practices.

6. The child-centered approaches to teaching (the micropractices) which characterized the first wave of progressivism of the 1930s to the mid-1960s influenced mainly preschool and primary school teachers (May, 1992a) and had little impact on pedagogy in secondary schools. However the "macrolevel" ideas of first-wave progressivism—that education can be the route to a democratic society—underpinned government policy and curricula for the post–war secondary schools. The micropractices, or pedagogy, associated with the neoprogressivism of the 1970s was more influential in secondary schools and drew on the radical social critiques of the 1960s for its political rationale. While the psychological underpinnings of first-wave progressivism had been Deweyan and psychoanalytic, those of the second wave were based on humanistic and behavioral psychology. In effect, secondary teachers took on board techniques which had long been characteristic of the primary school classroom, for example, individual and group work and field work in the wider community (Middleton, 1996d).

CHAPTER THREE

1. Conversations with Maori women and men have led me to believe that menstruation was not seen negatively, at least in certain tribes. As a Pakeha, I am unable to generalize about this. Pere (1988) commented of the Tuhoe and Ngati Kahungunu tribes that conception was not associated with sin, and menstrual blood was not seen as "the curse" or as pollution.

2. The term *nonmarital sex* avoids the ambiguity of *premarital sex*, which suggests that the couple later got married.

CHAPTER FOUR

1. I shall not use the binary *erotica/pornography* that is commonly used by feminists to distinguish between the permissable and the nonpermissable (McKinnon, 1989).

2. New legislation allowing prosecution of Internet providers who are accused of displaying objectional material.

3. Sec. 502, draft of United States Communications Decency Act of 1995, Information kindly supplied by the Center for Democracy and Technology, info@c-dt.org, via electronic transfer, March 16, 1996.

4. As this book went to press, the U.S. Supreme Court struck down the 1996 *U.S. Communications Decency Act*. On June 28, 1997, the Melbourne newspaper, *The Age*, quoted from the judgment as follows: "Notwithstanding the legitimacy and importance of the congressional goal of protecting children from harmful materials, we agree (with a lower court ruling) that the statute abridges the freedom of speech protected by the First Amendement of the Constitution," said the majority ruling. "The breadth of the restriction is unprecedented and the burden on adult freedom is not acceptable" (p. A18).

5. A former editor of *Harvard Law Review*, a feminist, and an activist in the American Civil Liberties Union.

6. Films and videos have each been classified under separate authorities. The new legislation brings films, videos, and printed publications under the same authority. The tribunal of which I was a member was responsible for printed publications only. I had nothing to do with the classification of films or videos.

7. The decision in which this test was formulated is decision No 1053. For a retrospective analysis of the origins of, and reasoning behind, this test see decision 4/91.

8. Author of *The Bone People*, which won the Booker Prize in 1983.

9. Appeals on tribunal decisions went to the High Court and were heard by a panel of three judges. In such an appeal in the High Court, Judge Jeffries had argued this in the decision *Re 'Fiesta' and 'Knave'* 1986 6 NZAR 213.

10. This definition was given earlier in this chapter.

11. New Zealand does not have a written constitution like that of the United States. Our Bill of Rights Act is very similar to the Canadian Charter.

12. This evidence is summarized in the tribunal's Decision 80/92.

References

Acker, S. (1994). *Gendered education*. Buckingham, England and Philadelphia: Open University Press.

Acker, S. (1995). Unkind cuts: Reflections on the U.K. university experience. *Ontario Journal of Higher Education 1995*, 55–74.

Aitken, J. (1996). Wives and mothers first: The New Zealand teachers' marriage bar and the ideology of domesticity, 1920–1940. *New Zealand Women's Studies Journal, 12*(1), 83–98.

Alther, L. (1976). *Kinflicks*. Harmondsworth, England: Penguin.

Althusser, L. (1971). Ideology and ideological state apparatuses. In L. Althusser (Ed.), *Lenin and philosophy* (pp. 127–186). London: Monthly Review Press.

Alton-Lee, A., & Densem, P. (1992). Towards a gender-inclusive school curriculum: Changing educational practice. In S. Middleton & A. Jones (Eds.), *Women and education in Aotearoa 2* (pp. 197–220). Wellington, New Zealand: Bridget Williams Books.

Apple, M. (Ed.) (1995–1996). *Review of Research in Education, 21*. Washington, DC: American Educational Research Association.

Apple, M. (1996a). *Cultural politics and education*. Buckingham, England: Open University Press.

Apple, M. (1996b). Power, meaning and identity in the United States. *British Journal of Sociology of Education, 17*(2), 125–142.

Arnot, M., & Weiler, K. (Eds.). (1993). *Feminism and social justice in education: International perspectives*. New York and London: Falmer Press.

Ball, S. (Ed.). (1990a). *Foucault and education: Discipline and knowledge*. London and New York: Routledge.

Ball, S. (1990b). Introducing Monsieur Foucault. In S. Ball (Ed.), *Foucault and education: Discipline and knowledge* (pp. 1–8). London and New York: Routledge.

Ball, S. (1994). *Education reform: A critical and post-structural approach*. Buckingham, England and Philadelphia: Open University Press.

Barrett, M. (1991). *The politics of truth: From Marx to Foucault*. Cambridge, England: Polity Press.

Barrington, J., & Beaglehole, T. (1974). *Maori schools in a changing society*. Wellington: New Zealand Council for Educational Research.

Barrington, R., & Gray, A. (1981). *The Smith women*. Wellington, New Zealand: Reed.

Beeby, C. E. (1986). Introduction. In W. E. Renwick, *Moving targets: Six essays on educational policy* (pp. xi–xiv). Wellington: New Zealand Council for Educational Research.

Beeby, C. E. (1992). *The biography of an idea: Beeby on education*. Wellington: New Zealand Council for Educational Research.

Bernstein, B. (1971). On the classification and framing of educational knowledge. In M.F.D. Young (Ed.), *Knowledge and control* (pp. 47–69). London: Collier McMillan.

Bhabha, H. (1994). *The location of culture*. London: Routledge.

Biklen, S. (1995). *School work: Gender and the cultural construction of teaching*. New York: Teachers College Press.

Bourdieu, P. (1971). Systems of education and systems of thought. In M.F.D. Young (Ed.), *Knowledge and control* (pp. 189–207). London: Collier Mc-Millan.

Brett, C. (1996, November). Sex and sensibility. *North and South*, 90–100.

Bunkle, P. (1979a, September). A history of the women's movement. (Part 1). *Broadsheet*, 24–28.

Bunkle, P. (1979b, October). A history of the women's movement. (Part 2). *Broadsheet*, 26–28.

Bunkle, P. (1979c, November). A history of the women's movement. (Part 3). *Broadsheet,* 26–28.

Bunkle, P. (1979d, December). A history of the women's movement. (Part 4). *Broadsheet,* 28–32.

Bunkle, P. (1980a, January/February). A history of the women's movement. (Part 5). *Broadsheet*, 30–35.

Bunkle, P. (1980b). The origins of the women's movement in New Zealand: The Women's Christian Temperance Union 1885–1995. In P. Bunkle & B. Hughes (Eds.), *Women in New Zealand society* (pp. 52–76). Auckland, New Zealand: Allen and Unwin.

Butler, J. (1993). *Bodies that matter*. Routledge: New York and London.

Carkeek, L., Davies, L., & Irwin, K. (1994). *What happens to Maori girls at school?* Wellington, New Zealand: Ministry of Education.

Casey, K. (1993). *I answer with my life: Life-histories of women teachers working for social change*. New York and London: Routledge.

Cazden, C. (1992). *Whole language plus: Essays on literacy in the United States and New Zealand*. New York: Teachers College Press.

Cherny, L., & Weise, E. R. (Eds.). (1996). *Wired women: Gender and new realities in cyberspace*. Seattle, WA: Seal Press.

Cheyne, C., & Ryan, A. (1989). *Submissions to the Committee of Inquiry into Pornography*. Palmerston North, New Zealand: Department of Sociology, Massey University.

Clandinin, J., & Connelly, F. M. (1995). *Teachers' professional knowledge landscapes*. New York: Teachers College Press.

Codd, J. (1996). Higher education and the Qualifications Framework: A question of standards. *Delta, 48*(1), 57–66.

Codd, J., Harker, R., & Nash, R. (Eds.). (1990). *Political issues in New Zealand education*. Palmerston North, New Zealand: Dunmore Press.

Connell, R. W., Ashenden, D. J., Kessler, S., & Dowsett, G. W. (1982). *Making the difference*. Sydney, Australia: Allen and Unwin.

Davies, B. (1989). *Frogs and snails and feminist tales*. Sydney, Australia: Allen and Unwin.

Davis, A. (1981). *Women, race and class*. London: Women's Press.

Day, B. (1992). Women in technical education: An historical account. In S. Middleton & A. Jones (Eds.), *Women and education in Aotearoa 2* (pp. 68–82). Wellington, New Zealand: Bridget Williams Books.

de Beauvoir, S. (1949/1971). *The second sex*. Harmondsworth, England: Penguin.

de Ras, M. (1996). [Review of the book *Nattering on the net: Women, power and cyberspace*]. *Women's Studies Journal, 12*(2), 135–137.

Department of Education. (1943). *The post-primary school curriculum* (Thomas Report). Wellington, New Zealand: Government Printer.

Department of Education. (1962). *Report of the Commission on Education in New Zealand* ("Currie Report"). Wellington, New Zealand: Government Printer.

Department of Education. (1976a). *Education and the equality of the sexes*. Wellington, New Zealand: Government Printer.

Department of Education. (1976b). *Towards partnership: Report of the Committee on Secondary Education* (McCombs Report). Wellington, New Zealand: Department of Education.

Department of Education. (1977). *Growing, sharing, learning: The report of the Committee on Health and Social Education* (Johnson Report). Wellington, New Zealand: Department of Education.

Department of Health. (1955). *Sex and the adolescent girl*. Wellington, New Zealand: Government Printer.

Donnerstein, E., Lintz, D., & Penrod, S. (1987). *The question of pornography*. New York: Free Press.

Donzelot, J. (1979). *The policing of families*. London: Hutchinson.

Dreyfus, H. L., & Rabinow, P. (Eds.). (1982). *Michel Foucault: Beyond structuralism and hermeneutics*. Chicago: Harvester.

Dugdale, D. F. (1994). The censorship we deserve. *Landfall* (187), 83–92.

Dworkin, A. (1981). *Pornography: Men possessing women*. London: Women's Press.

Education Review Office. (1996). *Reproductive and sexual health education. A report provided by the Education Review Office for the Ministry of Health*. Wellington, New Zealand: Education Review Office.

Ehrenreich, B., & English, D. (1979). *For her own good*. New York: Doubleday.

Eisenstein, Z. (1981). *The radical future of liberal feminism*. New York: Longman.

Eldred-Grigg, S. (1984). *Pleasures of the flesh: Sex and drugs in colonial New Zealand*. Wellington, New Zealand: Reed.

Elley, W. B. (1996). Unresolved issues in fitting academic courses into the Qualifications Framework. *Delta, 48*(1), 67–76.

Else, A. (1991). *A question of adoption*. Wellington, New Zealand: Bridget Williams Books.

Engels, F. (1891/1971). *The origin of the family, private property and the state*. New York: Pathfinder.

Fausto-Sterling, A. (1993, March/April). The five sexes: Why male and female are not enough. *The Sciences*, 20–24.

Ferguson, K. (1993). *The man question: Visions of subjectivity in feminist theory*. Berkeley: University of California Press.

Fine, M. (1988). Sexuality, schooling and adolescent females: The missing discourse of desire. *Harvard Educational Review, 58*(1), 29–53.

Firestone, S. (1979). *The dialectics of sex*. London: Women's Press.

Flax, J. (1990). *Thinking fragments*. Berkeley: University of California Press.

Flude, M., & Hammer, M. (Eds.). (1990). *The Education Reform Act, 1988: Its origins and implications*. London and New York: Falmer Press.

Foreman, A. (1977). *Femininity as alienation*. London: Pluto.

Foucault, M. (1977). *Discipline and punish: The birth of the prison*. Harmondsworth, England: Penguin.

Foucault, M. (1980a). *A history of sexuality* (Vol 1). New York: Vintage.

Foucault, M. (1980b). *Power/knowledge: Selected interviews and other writings 1972–1977* (C. Gordon, Ed.). New York: Pantheon.

Foucault, M. (1980c). *Heculine Barbin*. New York: Pantheon.

Foucault, M. (1982). Afterword: The subject and power. In H. L. Dreyfus & P. Rabinow (Eds.), *Michel Foucault: Beyond structuralism and hermeneutics*. Chicago: Harvester.

Frame, J. (1983). *To the is-land*. Auckland, New Zealand: Hutchinson.

Fraser, N. (1993). *Unruly practices: Power, discourse and gender in contemporary social theory*. Minneapolis: University of Minnesota Press.

Friedan, B. (1963). *The feminine mystique*. Harmondsworth, England: Penguin.

Fry, R. (1985). *It's different for daughters: A history of the curriculum for girls in New Zealand schools, 1900–1975*. Wellington: New Zealand Council for Educational Research.

Gavey, N. (1992). Technologies and effects of heterosexual coercion. *Feminism and psychology, 2*(3), 325–351.

Giddens, A. (1982). *Profiles and critiques in social theory*. London: Macmillan.

Gilbert, J. (1996). The sex education component of school science programmes as a "micro-technology" of power. *Women's Studies Journal, 12*(2), 37–58.

Glamuzina, J., & Laurie, A. (1991). *Parker and Hume: A lesbian view*. Auckland, New Zealand: New Women's Press.

Goodson, I. (Ed.). (1992). *Studying teachers' lives*. London: Routledge

Gordon, C. (1980). Afterword. In M. Foucault, *Power/knowledge: Selected interviews and other writings 1972–1977* (C. Gordon, Ed.). New York: Pantheon.

Grace, G. (1990). The New Zealand Treasury and the commodification of education. In S. Middleton, J. Codd , & A. Jones (Eds.), *New Zealand education policy today: Critical perspectives* (pp. 27–39). Wellington, New Zealand: Allen and Unwin/Port Nicholson Press.

Greene, M. (1986). In search of a critical pedagogy. *Harvard Educational Review, 56*, 427–441.

Greene, M. (1995). *Releasing the imagination*. San Francisco: Jossey-Bass.

Greer, G. (1971). *The female eunuch*. London: Granada.

Grosz, E. (1989). *Sexual subversions: Three French feminists*. Sydney, Australia: Allen and Unwin.

Grumet, M. (1988). *Bitter milk: women and teaching*. Amherst: University of Massachusetts Press.

Hansen, S., & Jensen, J. (1972). *The little red schoolbook*. Wellington, New Zealand: Alister Taylor.

Hanson, J. (1996). Learning to be a prostitute: Education and training in the New Zealand sex industry. *New Zealand Women's Studies Journal, 12*(1), 77–85.

Harding, S. (1987). *The science question in feminism*. Ithaca, NY: Cornell University Press.

Hartmann, H. (1981). The unhappy marriage of Marxism and feminism: Towards a more progressive union. In L. Sergent (Ed.), *Women and revolution* (pp. 1–42). Boston: South End.

Harvey, D. (1990). *The condition of postmodernity*. Cambridge, MA and Oxford, U.K.: Basil Blackwell.

Hennessey, R. (1993). *Materialist feminism and the politics of discourse*. New York and London: Routledge.

Henriques, J., Hollway, W., Urwin, C., Venn, C., & Walkerdine, V. (Eds.). (1984). *Changing the subject*. London: Methuen.

Hollway, W. (1984). Gender difference and the production of subjectivity. In J. Henriques, W. Hollway, C. Urwin, C. Venn, & V. Walkerdine (Eds.), *Changing the subject* (pp. 26–59). London: Methuen.

Holt, J. (1974). *How children fail*. Harmondsworth, England: Penguin.

Hoskin, K. (1990). Foucault under examination: The crypto-educationalist unmasked. In. S. Ball. (Ed.), *Foucault and education: Discipline and knowledge* (pp. 29–54). London and New York: Routledge.

Hughes, C., Lovell, T., Preston, R., & Martin, J. (1995). Editorial. *Gender and education, 7*(1), 3–8.

Indecent Publications Act. (1963). Wellington, New Zealand: Government Printer.

Indecent Publications Tribunal. (1992). *Submissions to the Select Committee on the Films, Videos and Publications Classifications Bill*. Wellington, New Zealand: Tribunals Division, Department of Justice.

Ingham, M. (1982). *Now we are thirty*. London: Methuen.

Irwin, K. (1990). The Politics of Kohanga Reo. In S. Middleton, J. Codd & A. Jones (Eds.), *New Zealand education policy today: Critical perspectives*. Wellington, New Zealand: Allen and Unwin/Port Nicholson Press.

Irwin, M. (1996). *Curricular confusion: The case for revisiting the New Zealand Curriculum Framework*. Paper presented at the seminar on Implementing the Curriculum, Principals' Centre, University of Auckland.

Jaggar, A. (1993, 18 August). *New Zealand Films, Videos and Publications Classification Act, 1992*. Paper presented to the New Zealand Society for Social and Legal Philosophy, Victoria University.

Jaggar, A., & Struhl, A. (Eds.). (1978). *Feminist frameworks*. New York: McGraw-Hill.

Johnson, J. (1973). *Lesbian nation: The feminist solution*. New York: Touchstone.

Jones, A. (1991). *At school I've got a chance. Culture/privilege: Pacific Islands and Pakeha girls at school*. Palmerston North, New Zealand: Dunmore.

Jones, A. (1992). Am 'I' in the text? In S. Middleton, & A. Jones (Eds.), *Women and education in Aotearoa 2* (pp. 18–32). Wellington, New Zealand: Bridget Williams Books.

Jones, A. (1993). Becoming a girl: Post-structural suggestions for educational research. *Gender and education, 5*(2), 157–166.

Jones, A., & Middleton, S. (Eds.). (1996). Educating sexuality. [Special issue]. *New Zealand Women's Studies Journal, 12*(1).

Jones, D. (1990). The genealogy of the urban schoolteacher. In S. Ball (Ed.), *Foucault and education: Discipline and knowledge* (pp. 57–77). London and New York: Routledge.

Jordan, J. (1991). *Working girls.* Auckland, New Zealand: Penguin.

Kappeler, S. (1986). *The pornography of representation.* Cambridge, England: Polity Press.

Kenway, J. (1990). Privileged girls, private schools, and the culture of success. In J. Kenway, & S. Willis (Eds.), *Hearts and minds: Self-esteem and the schooling of girls* (pp. 131–156). London: Falmer.

Kenway, J., Willis, S., Blackmore, J., & Rennie, L. (1993). Learning from girls: What can girls teach feminist teachers? In L. Yates (Ed.), *Feminism and education* (pp. 63–77). Melbourne, Australia: Melbourne Studies in Education, La Trobe University.

Khayatt, D. (1994). Surviving school as a lesbian student. *Gender and Education, 6* (1), 163–170.

Kirsch, G. E. (1995). Review: Critical pedagogy and composition. *College English, 6*(57), 723–729.

Klatch, R. (1987). *Women of the New Right.* Philadelphia: Temple.

Kohl, H. (1969). *The open classroom.* New York: New York Review.

Kristeva, J. (1986). *The Kristeva reader* (T. Moi, Ed.). New York: Columbia University Press.

Lather, P. (1990). *Getting smart.* New York and London: Routledge.

Lauder, H., & Wylie, C. (Eds.). (1990). *Towards successful schools.* London: Falmer.

Leahy, H. (1996). *Focusing on a fault line: Gender and education policy development in Aotearoa, New Zealand, 1975–1995.* Wellington: unpublished M. Ed. thesis, Victoria University.

Lees, S. (1993). *Sugar and spice: Sexuality and adolescent girls.* Harmondsworth, England: Penguin.

Lingard, B., Knight, J., & Porter, P. (Eds.). (1993). *Schooling reform in hard times.* London: Falmer Press.

Linn, E., Stein, N., Young, J., & Davis, S. (1992). Bitter lessons for all: Sexual harassment in schools. In James T. Sears (Ed.), *Sexuality and curriculum: The politics and practices of sexuality education* (pp. 106–123). New York: Teachers College Press.

Livingstone, D. (Ed.). (1987). *Critical pedagogy and cultural power.* South Hadley, MA: Bergin and Garvey.

Llewellyn, M. (1980). Studying girls at school: The impact of confusion. In R.

Deem (Ed.), *Schooling for women's work* (pp. 42–51). London: Routledge and Kegan Paul.

Luke, C. (1992). Feminist politics in radical pedagogy. In C. Luke and J. Gore (Eds.), *Feminisms and critical pedagogy* (pp. 25–53). New York and London: Routledge.

Luke, C. (1994). Women in the academy: The politics of speech and silence. *British Journal of Sociology of Education, 15*(2), 211–230.

Luke, C., & Gore, J. (Eds.). (1992a). *Feminisms and critical pedagogy.* New York and London: Routledge.

Luke, C., & Gore, J. (1992b). Women in the academy. In C. Luke, & J. Gore (Eds.), *Feminisms and critical pedagogy* (pp. 192–210). New York and London: Routledge.

Lyotard, J. (1984). *The postmodern condition.* Minneapolis: University of Minnesota Press.

Mac an Ghaill, M. (1994). *The making of men.* Buckingham, England and Philadelphia: Open University Press.

Mac an Ghaill, M. (1996). Sociology of education, state schooling and social class: Beyond critiques of the New Right hegemony. *British Journal of Sociology of Education, 17*(2), 163–174.

Macey, D. (1995). *The lives of Michel Foucault.* New York: Vintage.

Maher, F. A., & Tetreault, M. (1994). *The feminist classroom.* New York: Basic Books.

Marshall, J. (1990). Foucault and educational research. In S. Ball (Ed.), *Foucault and education: Discipline and knowledge* (pp. 11–28). London and New York: Routledge.

Martin, J. R. (1987). *Reclaiming a conversation: The ideal of the educated woman.* New Haven, CT: Yale University Press.

Marx, K. (1867/1976). *Capital. Vol. 1.* Harmondsworth, England: Pelican.

May, H. (1992a). Learning through play: Women, progressivism and early childhood education, 1920s–1950s. In S. Middleton, & A. Jones (Eds.), *Women and education in Aotearoa 2* (pp. 83–101). Wellington, New Zealand: Bridget Williams Books.

May, H. (1992b). *Minding children, managing men.* Wellington, New Zealand: Bridget Williams Books.

Mazengarb, O. C. (1954). *Report of the Special Committee on Moral Delinquency in Children and Adolescents* (Mazengarb Report). Wellington, New Zealand: Government Printer.

McDonald, D. (1978). Children and young persons in New Zealand society. In P. Koopman-Boyden (Ed.), *Families in New Zealand society* (pp. 44–56). Wellington, New Zealand: Reed.

McDonald, G. (1992). Are girls smarter than boys? In S. Middleton, & A. Jones (Eds.), *Women and education in Aotearoa 2* (pp. 102–121). Wellington, New Zealand: Bridget Williams Books.

McGeorge, C. (1981). Race and the Maori in the New Zealand school curriculum since 1877. *Australia and New Zealand Journal of History, 10,* 93–110.

McKenzie, D. (1975). The changing concept of equality in New Zealand education. In *New Zealand Journal of Education Studies, 10*(2), 93–110.

McKinnon, C. (1989). *Towards a feminist theory of the state.* Cambridge, MA: Harvard University Press.

McLeod, E. (1982). *Women working: Prostitution now.* London: Croom Helm.

McLuhan, M. (1964). *Understanding media.* London: Routledge and Kegan Paul.

McRobbie, A. (1978). Working-class girls and the culture of femininity. In Women's Studies Group (Ed.), *Women take issue* (pp. 96–108). Birmingham, England: Centre for Contemporary Cultural Studies/Hutchinson.

McWilliam, E. (1995). *In broken images: Feminist tales for a different teacher education.* New York: Teachers College Press.

McWilliam, E., & Jones, A. (1995). Eros and pedagogical bodies: The state of (non)affairs. In E. McWilliam & P. G. Taylor (Eds.), *Pedagogy, technology, and the body.* New York: Peter Lang.

Meadmore, D., & Symes, C. (1996). Of uniform appearance: A symbol of school discipline and governmentality. *Discourse, 17*(2), 209–226.

Mercurio, J. A. (1972). Corporal punishment in the school: The plight of the first year teacher. *New Zealand Journal of Educational Studies, 7*(2), 144–152.

Middleton, S. (1985). *Feminism and education in post-war New Zealand: A sociological analysis.* D. Phil. thesis, University of Waikato, Hamilton, New Zealand.

Middleton, S. (1987). Feminist academics in a university setting: A case study in the politics of educational knowledge. *Discourse, 8* (1), 25–47.

Middleton, S. (1987/1994). Schooling and radicalisation: Life-histories of New Zealand feminist teachers. *British Journal of Sociology of Education, 8*(2), 168–169. (Reprinted in *The education feminism reader* [pp. 279–299], by L. Stone, Ed., 1994. New York: Routledge.)

Middleton, S. (1988a). Dirty books and other secrets: Dilemmas of a feminist on the Indecent Publications Tribunal. *Sites* (17), 22–29.

Middleton, S. (1988b). A short adventure between school and marriage?: Contradictions in the education of the New Zealand 'post-war woman'. In S. Middleton (Ed.), *Women and education in Aotearoa* (pp. 72–88). *Vol 1.* Wellington, New Zealand: Allen and Unwin/Port Nicholson Press.

Middleton, S. (1992a). Equity, equality, and biculturalism in the restructuring of New Zealand schools: A life-history approach. *Harvard Educational Review, 62*(3), 301–322.

Middleton, S. (1992b). Gender equity and school charters: Some theoretical and political questions for the 1990s. In S. Middleton, & A. Jones (Eds.), *Women and education in Aotearoa 2* (pp. 1–17). Wellington, New Zealand: Bridget Williams Books.

Middleton, S. (1992c). Schooling and the reproduction of gender relations. In J. Lynch, C. Modgil, & S. Modgil (Eds.), *Equity or excellence?: Education and cultural reproduction* (pp. 99–116). London and Washington: Falmer Press.

Middleton, S. (1993a). *Educating feminists: Life-histories and pedagogy.* New York: Teachers College Press.

Middleton, S. (1993b). A post-modern pedagogy for the sociology of women's education. In M. Arnot, & K. Weiler (Eds.), *Feminism and social justice in education: International perspectives* (pp. 124–145). New York and London: Falmer Press.

Middleton, S. (1994). Sex, drugs and bombs: Six years on the Indecent Publications Tribunal. *Sites, 29*, 18–44.

Middleton, S. (1995). Doing feminist educational theory—A postmodernist perspective. *Gender and Education, 7*(1), 87–100.

Middleton, S. (1996a, April). *Canes, berets, and gangsta rap: Disciplining sexuality in school, 1920–1995.* Paper presented at the annual meeting of the American Educational Research Association, New York.

Middleton, S. (1996b). Doing qualitative educational research in the 1990s: Issues and practicalities. *Waikato Journal of Education, 2*, 1–23.

Middleton, S. (1996c, April). *Schools at war: Learning and teaching in New Zealand, 1939–1945.* Paper presented at the annual meeting of the American Educational Research Association, New York.

Middleton, S. (1996d). Towards an oral history of educational ideas in New Zealand as a resource for teacher education. *Teaching and Teacher Education, 12*(5), 543–560.

Middleton, S. (1996e). Uniform bodies?: Disciplining sexuality in school 1968–1995. *New Zealand Women's Studies Journal, 12*(2), 9–36.

Middleton, S., Codd, J., & Jones, A. (Eds). (1990). *New Zealand education policy today: Critical perspectives.* Wellington, New Zealand: Allen and Unwin/Port Nicholson Press.

Middleton, S., & May, H. (1997). *Teachers talk teaching 1915–1995: Early childhood, schools, teachers' colleges.* Palmerston North, New Zealand: Dunmore Press.

Miller, J. (1993). *The passion of Michel Foucault.* New York: Anchor.

Mills, C. W. (1959). *The sociological imagination.* Harmondsworth, England: Penguin.

Ministry of Education. (1988). *Tomorrow's schools.* Wellington, New Zealand: Government Printer.

Ministry of Education. (1993). *The New Zealand curriculum framework.* Wellington, New Zealand: Learning Media.

Mitchell, J. (1973). *Women's estate.* Harmondsworth, England: Penguin.

Morris, J., Haines, H., & Shallcrass, J. (1989). *Pornography: Report of the Ministerial Committee of Inquiry into Pornography.* Wellington, New Zealand: Committee of Inquiry into Pornography.

Morris, M., & Patton, P. (Eds.). (1979). *Michel Foucault: Power, truth, strategy.* Sydney, Australia: Feral.

Morss, J., & Linzey, T. (1991). *Growing up: The politics of human learning.* Auckland, New Zealand: Longman Paul.

Moynihan, C. (1992a, October 14). The normalisation of indecency. *New Zealand Tablet,* pp. 8–9.

Moynihan, C. (1992b, October 7). Who will control the censors? *New Zealand Tablet,* pp. 10–12.

Nash, R. (1993). *Succeeding generations: Family resources and access to education in New Zealand.* Auckland, New Zealand: Oxford University Press.

New Zealand Post-Primary Teachers' Association. (1969). *Education in change.* Auckland, New Zealand: Longman Paul.

New Zealand Treasury. (1987). *Government management: Vol 2. Education.* Wellington: Author.

Nicholson, L. (Ed.). (1990). *Feminism/postmodernism.* New York: Routledge.

O'Brien, M. (1982). Feminist theory and dialectical logic. In N. Keohane, M. Rosaldo, & B. Gelphi (Eds.), *Feminist theory: A critique of ideology* (pp. 99–112). Chicago: Harvester.

Olssen, E. (1981). Truby King and the Plunket Society: An analysis of a prescriptive ideology. *New Zealand Journal of History, 15*(1), 3–23.

Olssen, M. (Ed.). (1988). *Mental testing in New Zealand.* Dunedin, New Zealand: University of Otago Press.

O'Neill, A. (1992). Educational policy initiatives for girls: Are we included in the decent society? In H. Manson (Ed.), *New Zealand Annual Review of Education.* Wellington, New Zealand: Department of Education, Victoria University.

Openshaw, R. (1983). Saving femininity from the feminists: Some underlying assumptions of a New Zealand 'back to the basics' movement. *Discourse, 4*(2), 32–48.

Openshaw, R., Lee, G., & Lee, H. (1993). *Challenging the myths: Rethinking New Zealand's educational history.* Palmerston North, New Zealand: Dunmore.

Orange, C. (1989). *The Treaty of Waitangi.* Wellington, New Zealand: Allen and Unwin/Port Nicholson Press.

Orner, M. (1992). Interrupting the calls for student voice in "liberatory" education: A feminist poststructuralist perspective. In C. Luke & J. Gore (Eds.), *Feminisms and critical pedagogy* (pp. 74–89). New York and London: Routledge.

Paechter, C. (1996). Power, knowledge and the confessional in qualitative research. *Discourse, 17*(1), 75–84.

Paglia, C. (1995). *Vamps and tramps.* Harmondsworth, England: Penguin.

Papakura, M. (1983). *The old time Maori.* Auckland, New Zealand: New Women's Press.

Park, J. (Ed.). (1991). *Ladies a plate: Continuity and change in the lives of New Zealand women.* Auckland, New Zealand: Auckland University Press.

Parkinson, P. (1991). *The clammy palm.* Talk given at Victoria University.

Patton, P. (1979). Of power and prisons. In M. Morris, & P. Patton (Eds.), *Michel Foucault: Power, truth, strategy.* Sydney: Feral.

Pere, R. (1988). Te wheke: Whaia te maramatanga me te aroha. In S. C. Middleton (Ed.), *Women and education in Aotearoa* (pp. 6–19). Wellington, New Zealand: Allen and Unwin/Port Nicholson Press.

Perry, S. (1965). *The Indecent Publications Tribunal.* Christchurch, New Zealand: Whitcombe and Tombs.

Perry, S. (1980). *Indecent publications: Control in New Zealand.* Wellington, New Zealand: Government Printer.

Peters, M., & Marshall, J. (1996). The politics of curriculum: Busnocratic rationality and enterprise culture. *Delta, 48*(1), 33–46.

Piercy, M. (1983). *Braided lives*. Harmondsworth, England: Penguin.

Poster, M. (1990). *The mode of information: Poststructuralism and social context*. Chicago: Polity Press.

Poster, M. (1995). *The second media age*. New York and Cambridge, England: Polity Press/Basil Blackwell.

Postman, N., & Weingartner, C. (1971). *Teaching as a subversive activity*. Harmondsworth, England: Penguin.

Quinlivan, K. (1996). 'Claiming an identity they taught me to despise': Lesbian students respond to the regulation of same-sex desire. *Women's Studies Journal, 12*(2), 99–114.

Renwick, W. E. (1986). *Moving targets: Six essays on educational policy*. Wellington: New Zealand Council for Educational Research.

Rich, A. (1980). Compulsory heterosexuality and lesbian existence. *Signs, 5*(4), 631–660.

Ronai, C. (1992). The reflexive self through narrative: A night in the life of an erotic dancer/researcher. In C. Ellis, & M. Flaherty (Eds.), *Investigating subjectivity* (pp. 103–124). Newberry Park, CA: Sage.

Rose, G. (1993). *Feminism and geography: The limits of geographical knowledge*. Minneapolis: University of Minnesota Press.

Rout, B. (1992). Being staunch: Boys hassling girls. In S. Middleton, & A. Jones (Eds.), *Women and education in Aotearoa 2* (pp. 169–180). Wellington, New Zealand: Bridget Williams Books.

Rowbotham, S. (1973). *Woman's consciousness, man's world*. Harmondsworth, England: Penguin.

Ryan, A. (1988). The 'Moral Right', Sex Education and Populist Moralism. In S. Middleton (Ed.), *Women and education in Aotearoa* (pp. 114–126). *Vol 1*. Wellington, New Zealand: Allen and Unwin/Port Nicholson Press.

Said, E. (1993). *Culture and imperialism*. London: Vintage.

Sawicki, J. (1991). *Disciplining Foucault: Feminism, power and the body*. London: Routledge.

Scott, T. (1991). *Affidavit for Penthouse International. Submission to the Indecent Publications Tribunal*. Wellington, New Zealand: Tribunals Division, Department of Justice.

Sears, J. (1992a). Dilemmas and possibilities of sexuality education. In J. Sears, (Ed.), *Sexuality and curriculum: The politics of sexuality education* (pp. 7–33). New York: Teachers College Press.

Sears, J. (Ed.). (1992b). *Sexuality and curriculum: The politics of sexuality education*. New York: Teachers College Press.

Secada, W. (Ed.). (1989). *Equity in education*. London and New York: Falmer Press.

Segal, L., & McIntosh, M. (Eds.). (1992). *Sex exposed: Sexuality and the pornography debate*. London: Virago.

Seymour, R. (1981). *Women at stake: Ideological cross-currents in misogyny and philogyny*. D. Phil. thesis, Dept of Sociology, University of Waikato.

Sheridan, A. (1980). *Michel Foucault: The will to truth*. London and New York: Tavistock.

Shuker, R. (1987). *The one best system? A revisionist history of state schooling in New Zealand*. Palmerston North, New Zealand: Dunmore Press.

Sibley, D. (1995). *Geographies of exclusion*. London and New York: Routledge.

Silin, J. (1995). *Sex, death, and the education of children: Our passion for ignorance in the age of AIDS*. New York: Teachers College Press.

Smith, D. (1987). *The everyday world as problematic*. Boston: Northeastern University Press.

Smith, D. (1990). *The conceptual practices of power: A feminist sociology of knowledge*. Toronto: University of Toronto Press.

Smith, G. (1990). The politics of reforming Maori education: The transforming potential of Kura Kaupapa Maori. In H. Lauder & C. Wylie (Eds.), *Towards successful schooling* (pp. 183–197). London and New York: Falmer Press.

Smith, H. (1942). Your responsibility to public health. In YWCA (Ed.), *Relationships in war-time*. Wellington, New Zealand: YWCA.

Smith, L. (1993). Getting out from down under: Maori women, education, and the struggles for Mana Wahine. In M. Arnot, & K. Weiler (Eds.), *Feminism and social justice in education* (pp. 58–78). New York and London: Falmer Press.

Snook, I. (1996). The Education Forum and the curriculum framework. *Delta, 48*(1), 47.

Spender, D. (1982). Education: The patriarchal paradigm and the response to feminism. In D. Spender (Ed.), *Men's studies modified* (pp. 155–173). New York: Teachers College Press.

Spender, D. (1995). *Nattering on the Net: Women, power and cyberspace*. Melbourne, Australia: Spinifex.

Spivak, G. (1990). (S. Harasyn, Ed.). *The Post-colonial critic: Interviews, strategies, dialogues*. New York and London: Routledge

Stone, L. (Ed.). (1994). *Education feminism*. New York and London: Routledge.

Stoller, R. (1991). *Porn: Myths for the twentieth century*. New Haven, CT: Yale University Press.

Strossen, N. (1995). *Defending pornography: Free speech, sex, and the fight for women's rights*. New York: Doubleday.

Sturrock, F. (1993). *The status of girls and women in New Zealand education and training*. Wellington, New Zealand: Ministry of Education.

Taskforce to Review Educational Administration. (1987). *Administering for excellence* (Picot Report).Wellington, New Zealand: Ministry of Education.

Taylor, S. (1984). Reproduction and contradictions in schooling: The case of commercial studies. *British Journal of Sociology of Education, 5*(1), 3–18.

Te Awekotuku, N. (1992). Kia mau, kia manawanui—We will never go away: Experiences of a Maori lesbian feminist. In R. du Plessis et al. (Eds.), *Feminist voices: Women's studies texts for Aotearoa/New Zealand* (pp. 278–289). Auckland, New Zealand: Oxford University Press.

Tennant, M. (1986). Natural directions: The New Zealand movement for sexual differentiation in education during the early twentieth century. In B. Brookes et al. (Eds.). *Women in history: Essays on European women in New Zealand* (pp. 87–100). Wellington, New Zealand: Allen and Unwin/Port Nicholson Press.

Thompson, C. (1937/1971). *On women*. New York: Mentor.

Tolerton, J. (1992). *Ettie: a life of Ettie Rout*. Auckland, New Zealand: Penguin Books.

Trenchard, L., & Warren, H. (1987). Talking about school: The experiences of young lesbians and gay men. In G. Weiner & M. Arnot (Eds.), *Gender under scrutiny* (pp. 222–230). London: Hutchinson.

Trudell, B. (1992). Inside a ninth-grade sexuality classroom: The process of knowledge construction. In J. T. Sears (Ed.), *Sexuality and curriculum: The politics and practices of sexuality education* (pp. 203–225). New York: Teachers College Press

Tuana, N. (1989). The weaker seed. In N. Tuana (Ed.), *Feminism and science*. Indianapolis: Indiana University Press.

Tuohy, F., & Murphy, M. (1976). *Down under the plum trees*. Martinborough, New Zealand: Alister Taylor.

Verma, K. (Ed.). (1992). *Inequality and teacher education*. London: Falmer.

Walkerdine, V. (1984). Developmental psychology and the child-centred pedagogy: The insertion of Piaget into early childhood education. In J. Henriques et al. (Eds.), *Changing the subject* (pp. 153–202). London: Methuen.

Walkerdine, V. (1987). Sex, power and pedagogy. In M. Arnot & G. Weiner (Eds.), *Gender and the politics of schooling* (pp. 166–174). London: Hutchinson.

Walkerdine, V. (1992). Progressive pedagogy and political struggle. In C. Luke, & J. Gore (Eds.), *Feminisms and critical pedagogy* (pp. 15–24). New York and London: Routledge.

Walkerdine, V., & Lucey, H. (1989). *Democracy in the kitchen*. London: Virago.

Walkowitz, J. (1980). *Prostitution and Victorian society*. Cambridge, UK and New York: Cambridge University Press.

Watson, S. (1996). Hetero-sexing girls: 'Distraction' and single-sex schools. *Women's Studies Journal, 12*(2), 115–129.

Weedon, C. (1987). *Feminist practice and post-structuralist theory*. London: Basil Blackwell.

Weiler, K. (1988). *Women teaching for change: Gender, class and power*. New York: Bergin and Garvey.

Weiner, G. (1993). Shell-shock or sisterhood: English school history and feminist practice. In M. Arnot & K. Weiler (Eds.), *Feminism and social justice in education: International perspectives* (pp. 79–100). London and Washington, D.C.: Falmer Press.

Weiner, G. (1994). *Feminisms in education: An introduction*. Buckingham, England: Open University Press.

Whitehead, L. (1974). The Thomas report: A study in educational reform. In *New Zealand Journal of Educational Studies, 9*(1), 52–64.

Willis, P. (1977). *Learning to labour*. Westmead, UK: Saxon House.

Wilson, M. (1992). Towards a feminist jurisprudence in Aotearoa. In R. du Plessis, P. Bunkle, K. Irwin, A. Laurie, & S. Middleton (Eds.), *Feminist voices: Women's studies texts for Aotearoa/New Zealand* (pp. 266–277). Auckland, New Zealand: Oxford University Press.

Witherel, C., & Noddings, N. (Eds.). (1991). *Stories lives tell: Narrative and dialogue in education.* New York: Teachers College Press.

Women Against Pornography. (1989). *Activists' handbook.* Wellington, New Zealand: Author.

Wood, J. (1984). Groping towards sexism: Boys' sex talk. In A. McRobbie & M. Nava (Eds.), *Gender and generation* (pp. 55–84). London: Macmillan.

Yates, L. (1993a). *Education of girls: Policy, research and the question of gender.* Hawthorn, Victoria: Australian Council for Educational Research.

Yates, L. (1993b). Feminism and Australian state policy: Some questions for the 1990s. In M. Arnot, & K. Weiler (Eds.), *Feminism and social justice in education: International perspectives* (pp. 167–185). New York and London: Falmer Press.

Youth Voices (1996). Youth Voices. *Harvard Educational Review, 66*(2), 173–197.

Index

About the Author

Sue Middleton is author of *Educating Feminists: Life Histories and Pedagogy* (Teachers College Press). Sue has published widely in the United States and Britain, as well as in her home country, New Zealand. She teaches, writes, and researches on topics related to education policy, educational theory, qualitative research (especially life history) methods, and sexuality. Of particular interest are experimental, reflexive, modes of writing in the education disciplines. Sue is Assistant Dean, Graduate Studies, in the School of Education at the University of Waikato, Hamilton, New Zealand. She loves to travel, adores jazz, is married, and has a twenty-year-old daughter.